Eco Kids

SELF-SUFFICIENCY HANDBOOK

The greatest gifts you can give your children are the roots of responsibility and the wings of independence.

—Denis Waitley, American motivational speaker (1933–)

Eco Kids

SELF-SUFFICIENCY HANDBOOK

STEAM Projects to Help Kids Make a Difference

ALAN & GILL BRIDGEWATER

Happy Fox BOOKS

Eco Kids Self-Sufficiency Handbook is an original work, first published in 2019 by Fox Chapel Publishing Company, Inc. Reproduction of its contents is strictly prohibited without written permission from the rights holder.

ISBN 978-1-64124-030-7

Library of Congress Cataloging-in-Publication Data

Names: Bridgewater, Alan, author. | Bridgewater, Gill, author.
Title: Eco kids self-sufficiency handbook / Alan and Gill Bridgewater.
Description: Mount Joy, PA : Happy Fox Books, an imprint of Fox Chapel
   Publishing Company, Inc., [2019] | Audience: Age 7-14. | Includes index.
Identifiers: LCCN 2018035061 | ISBN 9781641240307 (pbk.)
Subjects: LCSH: Environmental protection--Citizen participation--Juvenile
   literature. | Environmental responsibility--Juvenile literature.
Classification: LCC TD171.7 .B744 2019 | DDC 363.7/0525--dc23
LC record available at https://lccn.loc.gov/2018035061

To learn more about the other great books from Fox Chapel Publishing, or to find a retailer near you, call toll-free 800-457-9112 or visit us at *www.FoxChapelPublishing.com*.

We are always looking for talented authors. To submit an idea, please send a brief inquiry to acquisitions@foxchapelpublishing.com.

Fox Chapel Publishing makes every effort to use environmentally friendly paper for printing.

Printed in Singapore
First printing

All photos and illustrations provided by the authors except where noted below.
Shutterstock photos: Cover: John Roman Images (inset left), Hatchapong Palurtchaivong (inset center), A3pfamily (inset right), Sunny studio (main); ii: Sunny studio; v: Maxx-Studio (background); 6 (bottom left), 119: Poznyakov; 6 (bottom right), 152: Georgina198; 7, 84: MaraZe; 9: Romrodphoto; 10: Halfpoint (right); 11: EvgeniiAnd (left), Alena Ozerova (right); 13: Jacob_09; 14: Pressmaster; 18: Richard P Long; 27: Luis Louro (bottom); 19: IrinaK; 32: sasaperic (right), Nate Allred (left); 37: kakteen; 39: Gladskikh Tatiana; 47: Mary Terriberry; pgs. 48–49: Diyana Dimitrova; 50: Nitr; 54: BaselineWorks; 55: gorillaimages; 57: Fotofermer (right); 59: Titisak Wangkasem; 60: Martien van Gaalen; 61: 000; 62: Foodpictures; 69: gorillaimages; 71: TukkataMoji (top right), napocska (bottom), nikkytok (top left); 72: EF Photography; 77: donatas1205 (top); 78: Hortimages; 80: freeskyline; 81: aboikis; 82: TheLiftCreativeServices; 83: Stacyann105 (top), Nataly Studio (bottom); 85: annielimdesign (bottom right), Tatiana_Didenko (bottom left), Tanja Esser (top left); 86: B Brown; 87: Jeff Wilson (top), sirtravelalot (center), Aquir (bottom); pgs. 88–89: palidachan; 95: CL-Medien; 101, back cover (bottom): Trong Nguyen; 102: Benedek Alpar; 103: Serg64; 104: Zurijeta; 106: amenic181; 109: Olesia Bilkei; 110: Alessandro Pietri (top), Kevin Key (bottom); 111: Alexander Image (top), Joseph Sorrentino (bottom); pgs. 116–117: Christine Glade; 121: Dmitry Galaganov; 124: Graeme Dawes; 125: JueWorn; 127: Fotos593; 128: GOLFX (top), Paolo Bona (bottom); 129: Mr Doomits (top), science photo (bottom); 131: Monkey Business Images; 132: Lapina (top), Brian A. Jackson (bottom); 133: Dasha Rosato; 135: Monkey Business Images; 137: Hans Christiansson; 138: Photo_works; 139: altanaka; 144: Lunov Mykola; 145: Neil Lockhart; 146: Reid Dalland; 147: Richard Evans (top right), Olga Vasilyeva (middle right), Volurol (bottom right), A. L. Holmes (bottom left); 148: Chamille White; 151: kalavati (top), Frank1Crayon (bottom); 157: Helen Hotson; 158: roibu; 159: John Roman Images.
Tool icons on 8, 10, 11, and 15: Shutterstock/Moofer.
iStock images: 26 (bottom left), 38, 74, 77 (center right), 118, 155.
Take Eco Action graphic, notebook graphic (61), and abstract triangles graphics designed by Freepik (Freepik.com).
Hand icons and happy/sad face icons courtesy of Flaticon.com.
Sky background (cover) courtesy of pngtree.com
Grass letter filling in title (cover, pages i and iii) courtesy of FreeArtBackgrounds.com.
The authors would like to give a big thank you to the children who participated in the making of this book: Charlotte, Hamish, and Isobel Roberts, Terri Hill, and Harley and Jessica Bridgewater. Thanks also to the students and teachers of Esher School for the photo of the Eco Bike Trailer (page 123).

Safety Advice

Adults must not allow children to use ladders unsupervised, dangerous tools or be near dangerous structures and hazardous conditions. We recommend that children only be allowed to use a hammer, a handsaw and a cordless drill/driver and only when a loving, caring and responsible adult is supervising them. Adults using tools and ladders must follow the manufacturer's instructions for safe operation (wear a dust mask and eye protection if instructed to do so). Adults must not operate dangerous power tools with children nearby. Every project has a safety rating indicated by the following symbols.

ASK AN ADULT TO HELP:
The project uses dangerous tools; an adult must do the dangerous bits and kids must be supervised at all times.

BE CAREFUL:
The project needs adult supervision at all times.

ALWAYS ASK:
Kids should check with an adult before using the tools and materials.

TABLE OF CONTENTS

How to Use Tools Safely and Properly

The most important points to remember are not to allow children to use dangerous tools and always follow the tool manufacturers' operating instructions. Below is a list of tools used and how to use them safely and effectively.

COMPASSES
A two-legged tool used for scribing and marking circles and radii. In use, set the legs a certain distance apart, spike one leg down on the workpiece, and then scribe the arc, circle, or step-off.

CORDLESS DRILL/DRIVER
Used for drilling holes and driving in screws. Safe (low voltage) and good for remote locations. For drilling, set the tool to drilling mode, fit the appropriate drill bit, and drill the hole, ensuring your free hand is away from the drill bit. For small holes use twist bits and for large holes (above ½ in. [10 mm]) use flat bits. For driving in screws, set the tool to screwing mode and the lowest speed and choose a torque setting. The torque setting (numbers dialed by rotating the end "chuck" of the tool) is a function to avoid over tightening the screws; a low number uses very little power for small screws and a high number uses more power for larger screws. The tool stops driving and starts clicking when the torque setting has been applied.

DARNING NEEDLE
A blunt-ended needle with a big eye used with thick thread for hand sewing. In use yarn or thread is passed through the eye and the needle is threaded in and out of the fabric.

GARDENING TROWEL
A small handheld digging tool. Used for digging small holes in soil.

HAMMER
Used for driving in pins and nails. A claw on the back of the hammer is used for extracting nails. The nail is held between finger and thumb, and gently tapped with the hammerhead until the nail supports itself, the supporting hand is then removed, and the nail is driven home.

HAND-AXE
Used to shape wood. **Do not allow children to use this tool.** In use, the tool is held in one hand and swung so the blade cuts the wood.

HANDSAW
A general-purpose saw for cutting straight lines in wood. The saw is held with one hand, the blade is aligned with the cut line, and is pushed and pulled.

JIGSAW

A powered saw with a thin blade for cutting straight lines and curves in thin-section wood. **Do not allow children to use this tool.** In action, the blade is aligned with the line of cut, the power is switched on, and the tool is advanced.

KITCHEN KNIFE

Used for cutting insulation board. A saw-toothed knife is a safer option. Held in one hand and used like a saw.

KNITTING NEEDLE

Used in pairs for knitting wool. Choose the right size of needle for the thickness of wool. In use, the needles are held one in each hand and are used to hook and knot the wool.

MEZZALUNA

A two-handed knife used for chopping herbs and so on. Inherently safe since it is held with both hands. In use the tool is held with both hands and the food is cut with a chopping, rocking motion.

PAINTBRUSH

Used for applying paint and varnish. Instructions for using paint and cleaning brushes are found on the paint can.

SANDPAPER

Abrasive paper used for smoothing wood. In use, the paper is supported on the hand or around a block and worked back and forth in a scrubbing motion.

SEWING MACHINE

Used for sewing fabrics. Follow the manufacturers' instructions.

SLEDGEHAMMER

A long handled heavy hammer for banging in posts, breaking rubble, and compacting earth. **Do not allow children to use this tool.** In use, the handle is gripped in both hands and the tool is swung so the head strikes the post, rubble, or earth.

SPADE

Use for digging holes in the ground. In use the handle is held and maneuvered by both hands,

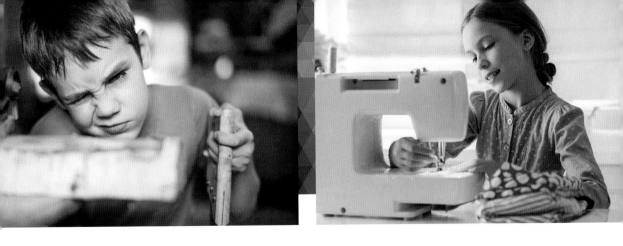

the metal blade is positioned where you want to dig, and one foot is used to push down on the top of the blade.

SPANNER
Used for adjusting nuts and bolts. Choose a spanner to fit the nut or bolt, place it on the nut or bolt, and rotate to loosen or tighten.

LEVEL
A testing tool to check that your work is horizontal or vertical. The absolute level is indicated by the bubble. In use, the tool is positioned on the workpiece at which point the workpiece is adjusted until the bubble is centered between two lines.

LADDER
A portable ladder consisting of a hinged frame with a small platform at the top. Has to be placed on a firm, level surface. **Take extreme caution if allowing children to use a ladder.** In use, the ladder is opened, positioned, and set level.

TAPE MEASURE
Flexible steel, retractable ruler used for measuring. Another fabric version is used for sewing projects. In use, the zero end is positioned, the tape measure is extended along the workpiece, and a mark is made or a measurement is taken.

TRY-SQUARE
Use for testing lines and edges are at right angles (90°) to each other. In use, the wooden stock is held hard up against the edge of the workpiece and a line is drawn along the edge of the steel blade.

T-SQUARE
Similar to a try-square but much larger.

WHEELBARROW
A one-wheeled cart used for moving soil and other heavy loads. In use, the barrow is filled, the handles are lifted, and the barrow is pushed along. The contents can be tipped out of the front.

Introduction

What Is Eco Kids Self–Sufficiency?

If as a kid you can do things like build a camp, light a fire, cook out in the open, sleep under the stars, fix your bike, grow your own vegetables, and keep chickens for eggs, then you are well on the way to becoming independent, or "self-sufficient," which means you don't have to rely on other people. Where it gets really exciting is that, if you can build a self-sufficient world in miniature, then when you are older you will be able to confidently shape and build your adult world.

Why Should We Care about the Environment?

If you imagine yourself travelling out into space and looking down at our world from a distance, you'll see that all the things we know—our homes, families, friends, food, forests, animals, rivers, and seas—are down here on Earth. If we believe just a little bit of what we read and see on the TV, and if we take it as fact that our "Mother Earth" is sick, stressed out, and generally very unhappy, then it's plain to see that we must begin to look after our wildlife, care for our plants, reduce pollution, and generally clean up our way of living. Think about it—if Mother Earth is all we have, and there's nowhere else to go, we simply have no other choice than to look after our environment very carefully.

The world is
a fine place
and worth the
fighting for.

— Ernest Hemingway, American Lost
Generation novelist (1899–1961)

How You Can Help Improve the World

First things first—there's no need for you to get stressed and anxious about eco issues. Things like pollution are important and real, and we do need to make huge changes, but the fact that these problems are real means that we can use muscle-and-brain solutions to sort them out. In the same way as you can keep your bedroom clean by taking off your shoes before you enter it—so that the floor doesn't get covered in muddy footprints—we all need to make a number of small changes so that we move through everyday life without leaving a line of filthy, waste-covered, pollution-smeared, carbon-heavy "footprints."

If you show your friends that your eco-conscious, self-sufficient lifestyle is not only a fun adventure, but also an ongoing mission to explore issues such as growing food, recycling, and generally being less reliant on faraway industrial companies, then you are in a way showing your friends how it's possible to care for the whole world. Your self-sufficient, "eco-warrior" efforts will set off a chain reaction that will eventually change things for the better.

What is STEAM?

STEAM—Science, Technology, Engineering, Arts, and Math—is a new way of thinking about education in which different school subjects are taught at once instead of separately. It's an update to the earlier STEM, which many education experts felt left out the arts at the risk of developing less caring, less creative students. What we all know is that the world will always need caring people who can think creatively and across disciplines to solve problems. In short, STEAM means learning by *doing*—getting your hands dirty, figuring out how things work—and this book will guide you through many projects that do just that. Remember, it's always more fun if you work with your friends, brothers and sisters, and parents. Read below to see how the STEAM guide works, and when you're ready to begin your adventures in eco self-sufficiency, pick a project, and get started!

 **SCIENCE**

TECHNOLOGY

 ENGINEERING

ARTS

 MATH

Picnic Table, page 32

Using the STEAM Guide

This helpful graphic guide shows you which of the five STEAM skills you will need to use more than the others to complete a given project. The higher the bar over the letter, the more important that skill is for that project. For example, the above icon shows that engineering skills—those needed to design and build something—are going to be used the most. It makes sense because you start with pieces of wood and end up with a table! You will need a little bit of artistic skill since the project involves craftsmanship, and you'll be using basic math, but science and technology play less of a role in this rustic woodworking endeavor.

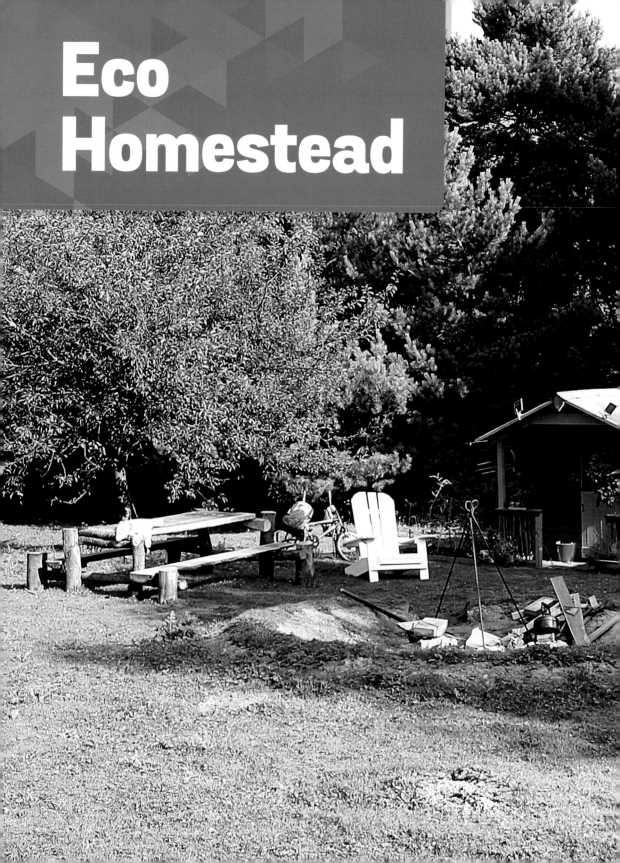

Eco Homestead

All life is an experiment. The more experiments you make the better.

—Ralph Waldo Emerson, American Transcendentalist philosopher and writer (1803–1882)

Eco Den

An eco den is a sort of mix between an old shack in the woods, a small gypsy caravan, a canal boat, a tree house, and a self-contained space pod. The aim is to build a self-sufficient hideout using mostly recycled materials—a place where you and your friends can hang out and do your own thing. An adult will need to help you with this project.

Fun, exciting, and challenging to build, a finished eco den is cozy and private, and it's a place where you can hang out with your friends or invite them for a sleepover. It's good for quiet reading and for doing your homework—basically it's a place where you can do exactly what you want, when you want.

To get started, you'll need to get an old shed.

If you look in your local newspaper or online, you'll see that there are lots of old sheds free for collection. Our shed was a complete mess—every wall and floor panel was in some way broken. All we did was patch it up with thrown-away materials. The biggest costs were for the metal sheets for the roof, and for the hundreds of screws and nails.

Measuring lengths, diagonals, and angles, checking for level, and ensuring foundation, walls, and roof all tie in together perfectly—basically constructing a little building—will put you through the paces of structural engineering. Then at the end you'll perform the duties of interior decorator.

What You'll Need . . .

- An old shed
- Salvaged concrete blocks or slabs
- Tape measure and level
- Slab, tile, or slate for shims/packing pieces
- Joists about 4 x 4 in. (10 x 10 cm)
- Roofing felt
- Screws, nails, fencing staples, and roofing screws, sizes and quantity to fit your salvaged materials
- Cordless drill/driver and bits
- Hammer
- Salvaged wood for repairs and additions (depending on your shed condition and design)
- Handsaw
- 2 G-clamps
- Chicken wire, enough to wrap around the base of the shed once
- Ladder
- Insulation board, enough to cover the roof and the walls
- Roof battens (thin sticks of wood) 1½ x ¾ in. (4 x 2 cm), enough to cover your roof at 18 in. (46 cm) intervals
- Salvaged plastic window
- Corrugated metal roofing sheet, enough to cover the roof with approximately 3 in. (7 cm) overlaps and in a length that overhangs your shed by at least 4 in. (10 cm)
- Metal roofing ridge strip, enough to cover your shed with approximately 3 in. (7 cm) overlaps
- Sealant
- Leftover paint and paintbrushes
- Wheelbarrow

1. Have a look at your yard or garden and talk to your family, then ask yourself what sort of den you are aiming for. Also, where is the den going to be built?

2. Search for a shed that you like and dismantle into panels. Measure the length and width of your shed. If it's going on a level, paved patio then you can skip the next step.

3. Set concrete blocks/slabs directly on the ground at each corner so that they match up with the size and shape of your shed floor panel(s). Check that your layout has 90° corners by measuring the diagonals with a tape measure (the distance between opposite corners). Make adjustments until both diagonals are equal. If you fail to achieve 90° corners the shed will be skewed and crooked. Place more blocks at regular intervals for supporting the joists—these are strong pieces of wood, about 4 x 4 in. (10 x 10 cm), that support all the weight, and they need to be spaced about 16 in. (40 cm) apart. Use shims or "packing pieces" (slab, tile, or slate) laid on top of the blocks/slabs to make them level with each other (use a level to check, see page 11 for how to do this).

4. Lay out the joists and slide pieces of roofing felt between the wooden joists and the blocks/slabs to stop dampness.

3

Concrete blocks/slabs support the joists and floor panels.

4

Put roofing felt between the blocks/slabs and the joists.

Why Is It Important to Reuse and Recycle?

"Eco" or "eco-friendly" means doing things in a way that doesn't hurt nature, and "recycling" means converting unwanted materials into something new, so an eco den is built using "salvaged" (found) or recycled materials in a way that doesn't damage the environment. We used an old window, leftover paint, a mixture of leftover and salvaged wood, and other "rubbish" that would otherwise have been wasted.

Reusing or recycling as many things as possible keeps goods and materials out of our landfills, which are rapidly becoming full up. Because we then don't need so many new things, it also saves energy, reduces the strain on natural resources, creates less pollution, saves money, and generally makes for a much more clean and comfortable life for everyone.

6

5. Lift the floor panels into place and attach them with screws or nails. This is heavy and tricky, so you'll need help.

6. Using the level floor panels as a workbench, put the wall panels down on it and use a hammer to remove rotten wood and remove any rusty nails.

7. Measure the lengths of wood that need replacing. Transfer the measurements through to the new wood and use the saw to cut them to size. Nail the "patches" carefully in place. Be careful to avoid hurting your hands on splinters and sharp nails—you may want to wear work gloves.

Repairing rotten wood.

Support the wood at a convenient height and get someone to hold it down firmly as you saw.

8. If you need to mend the frame, cut out the rotten sections, cut new sections to fit in the gaps, and screw them in place. Use extra bits of wood to bridge across the mends.

9. Use G–clamps to fix the position of the four wall panels in place on the floor panel, and carefully screw them firmly to the floor and to each other. Add battens ("trim") to the four outside corners of the shed.

10. Use chicken wire wrapped around the base of the shed, stapled in place and buried 12 in. (30 cm) in the ground to prevent animals from burrowing under the shed.

11. You'll need help to lift the roof panels in place—make sure they are well situated and aligned and attach them with screws driven through into the top edge of the wall. Screw adjoining roof panels together at the ridge (from inside the shed).

Add corner trim.

12

12. Carefully cut the insulation to fit, cover the insulation with the roofing felt, and attach with roof battens nailed securely to the roof as seen in the photo.

13. Here, a plastic window found on a dumpster was used to replace the broken window. Attach with screws.

Roof detail.

13

Install the window.

Why Is Insulation So Important?

If you skip a layer of insulation, your den will be icy cold in the winter and baking hot in the summer. You will then have to waste loads of money on either heating or cooling it so that it is nice to spend time in.

Insulating materials such as wool, fiberglass, compressed paper, and processed plant fibers are winners on two counts—they are less expensive than high-cost energy, and their use saves more energy— and more money. In fact, when it comes to insulation and saving energy, the very best option would be to wrap your house up in wool and bury it in the ground under a layer of living grass. You can't get warmer or cooler than that, because wool and grass are both excellent insulating materials.

What Can You Use to Insulate Your Den?

You can line the walls inside your den with fiberglass loft insulation (always wearing a mask, overalls, and gloves) or insulation board. You can also use old wool blankets, corrugated cardboard, or straw, covered with thin sheets of recycled plywood. If your window isn't double-glazed, why not have thick curtains? Keep icy blasts out with a long, sausage-shaped pillow at the bottom of the door (stuff old pant legs with rags, and then tie the ends round with string).

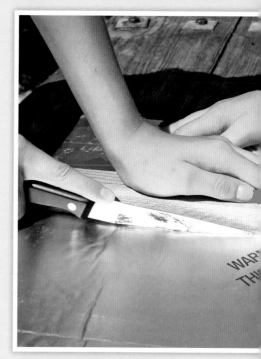

Cut the insulation board to size.

Its wool keeps a sheep warm in winter and cool in summer.

Cover the insulation with plywood.

Cover all the walls with insulation.

These earthy Icelandic houses are perfectly insulated.

14. We decided to extend the roof and make an area of decking at the front by removing the turf, placing extra joists level with the floor of the shed, decking the joists, and using posts and battens to create a support structure for the added roof. The main part of this structure is an A–frame that is the same shape as the roof. Join the bits of wood with screws or nails and then cut to length as shown in the picture.

15. Screw the corrugated roofing sheets in place using roofing screws.

16. Attach a metal ridge strip to cover the join at the top of the roof using roofing screws.

15

14

16

How Off-Grid Can You Go?

A truly self-sufficient, off-grid setup—a home, village, town, or city—would produce all its own food, swap things, create its own energy, and clean up its own waste.

The off-grid part will really depend upon where you live, and on how much time and effort you're going to put in. We have built a rain-collector for water, as well as a wind turbine and a solar panel for lights, but we also have to go back to the house for some water, and to use the toilet. You also might want to build a solar oven for simple cooking.

What Does "Off-Grid" Mean?

An off-grid house—it could be your den—finds its own water and creates its own energy without tapping into the normal, "on-grid" supplies of water, gas, oil, and electricity. An off-grid home uses non-fossil energy such as wind and solar power.

TIP:

Add a solar panel! (See page 96.)

17. Add other decorative details to your shed in whatever way you like. We added a rustic balustrade and decking at the front but you could take inspiration from the materials you have salvaged.

18. Finally, when you have finished applying decorative details, seal any gaps with sealant (particularly around the window). Paint the walls and doors inside and out in the colors of your choice (we used odds and ends of leftover paint). Be on the lookout for some chairs and extra furniture.

How Different Can Your Den Be?

Your den can be very different from ours. The shape will be decided by your found shed, and its character will be shaped by the color, the size, the nature of your salvaged materials, and your interests. Bigger, smaller, lower, higher, with more windows, a different roof, a bigger porch—your den can be anything that strikes your fancy. Here are some ideas.

Decorate the inside of the den however you like!

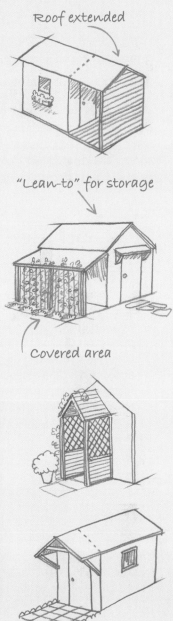

Roof extended

"Lean-to" for storage

Covered area

Picnic Table

This project is great because it only uses recycled wood. The posts came from a pile of wood we had put aside for logs, the top was an old door we found washed up on a beach, and the seat boards were a pair of scraps from the local sawmill. When sourcing your own free wood, keep in mind that it depends on where you live.

You could maybe try a river or a beach for driftwood, shops that sell motorcycles for packing cases, sawmills for sawn scraps, or a local builder who may have non-returnable pallets and old wood or spare lumber to dispose of. Always check that it's OK to salvage the wood, and watch out for any sharp nails sticking out! Before you start, ask an adult to help you with this project. The wood is quite heavy and tools like the hand-axe are very dangerous so must only be used by an adult.

After figuring out how you want your table to look, you'll need to creatively source found wood, and from there you'll be measuring, using tools, and joining pieces of wood together. Using hand tools, thinking about appearances, and repeating measurements come together to help you make something that your friends and family will enjoy for many years.

Nothing's better than a picnic!

— Zooey Deschanel, American actress and singer (1980–)

What You'll Need . . .

- Salvaged door to make a tabletop about 82 in. (210 cm) long, 30 in. (75 cm) wide, with two seats about 87 in. (220 cm) long, 12 in. (30 cm) wide
- 4 sticks for marking out
- Spade
- Green wood (with bark on it): 8 poles each at 100 in. (254 cm) long
- Tape measure
- Handsaw and hand-axe
- Hammer and 6 in. (15 cm) nails

1. Lay your found tabletop on the grass where you want the table, mark its position with four sticks, and start by digging 8 holes in the ground, 12 in. (30 cm) deep for the vertical posts. The seat postholes need to be 21 in. (53 cm) away from the table leg posts. Cut 4 table leg posts 40 in. (102 cm) long, and 4 seat posts 26 in. (66 cm) long.

2. Set the eight posts in the ground—4 at each end—replace dirt around the poles and use your foot to stomp the dirt down. Measure and carefully cut horizontal bars to fit across the posts and nail them in place as shown. The lengths of these bars will vary dramatically depending on your materials.

Lay all the parts out on the grass.

2

Nail the long bars to the posts.

3

Cut flat areas to make a good fit.

3. When you're working with poles, always make sure when nailing one part to another that they come right together for a good, close fit. Use the handsaw and hand-axe (remember, only adults must use the hand-axe) to create some flat areas so that the logs will fit together snugly.

4. Bridge the tabletop and seat planks over the horizontal bars and nail in place. Nail the seat planks in place at either side of the table.

5. Fix each seat plank so the straightest edge is facing the table. This is so the sitters can sit down without scratching the back of their legs.

More Picnic Table Ideas

Planks screwed to cross pieces

Additional wood to reinforce the structure

Legs buried in ground

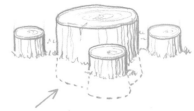

Large logs buried in the ground

What Is Deforestation, and How Can You Help Prevent It?

Deforestation is the destruction, clearing, and removal of our forests. This kills wildlife, reduces oxygen, damages the soil, pollutes the atmosphere, causes flooding, and generally messes up our world. But whenever you reuse or recycle paper, cardboard, or wood you are helping to slow down deforestation. The more paper we recycle, the more solid wood we recycle and/or use as fuel, and the more we stop sawing down trees, the longer our forests will last.

Every ton of recycled paper saves 17 trees from being cut down. The USA cuts down 68 million trees a year to make about 65 billion pieces of junk mail. Why don't we use more recycled paper and say no to junk mail?

Campfire Circle

A campfire circle, which my grandfather used to describe as a "cowboy campfire," is an area where you can have a fire and do your cooking in relative safety. The circle is made up of a central pit (to contain the fire and stop it from spreading), an inner ring of large stones, and an outer raised ring of turf. The idea is that you sit on the raised ring with your feet braced against the stones. This way, you can cook without coming to any harm.

Putting geometry skills to use, you'll measure out a large circle, and then shape an area of earth to fit your s'mores-roasting needs. Aside from creating a warm place to share ghost stories, you'll have the chance to cook food the same way cowboys did.

The fire is the main comfort of the camp, whether in summer or winter.

— Henry David Thoreau, American Transcendentalist writer and naturalist (1817–1862)

What You'll Need ...

- Rope and two poles
- Bricks and large stones
- Garden tools
- Sledgehammer

1. Use a length of rope and two found poles, like our batten and iron rod, and mark or "scribe" out a 120 in. (305 cm) diameter circle. (The rope, when tied to the poles, should be half this length to create the right size of circle.)

2. Clear the turf with a garden spade and put it around the edge so as to make a raised ring or hump.

3. Take earth from the center of the ring and from other areas in the garden and use it to pad out the ring on both sides—so that you finish up with a big saucer shape. Dig away a small bit for the entrance.

4. Dig out a central pit, about 18 in. (45 cm) deep and 24–35 in. (60–90 cm) in diameter, and fill it up with bricks. Ask an adult to use a sledgehammer to break the bricks into small pieces (see page 10).

5. Use bricks to build little supports around the central pit, so that you have somewhere to rest cooking pans. Place the large stones around the edge of the pit.

Mark out the circle and remove the turf (steps 1–2).

3

Digging an entrance.

4

Place extra earth around the ring and smooth it out.

Adirondack Chair

An Adirondack chair is a comfortable outdoor chair that you can easily make from recycled wood. It was originally a sort of roughly built chair, homemade by poor people in the Adirondack Mountains region of the USA. Next time you see a film that shows American mountain folk sitting around on a porch, have a close-up look at the chairs—they could well be Adirondacks.

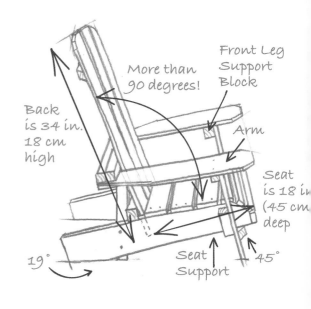

More than 90 degrees!

Front Leg Support Block

Arm

Back is 34 in. 18 cm high

Seat is 18 in. (45 cm) deep

Seat Support

19°

45°

This is a fairly complex woodworking project that requires lots of measuring, cutting, and fastening. Once the chair is built, it's time to paint and/or decorate, and then it's time to laze the day away in one of the most comfortable chair designs of all time.

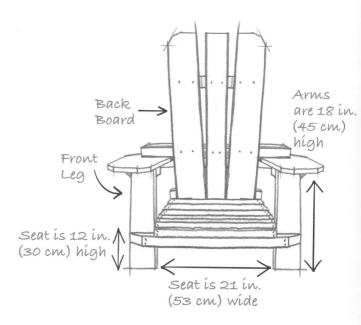

Back Board

Arms are 18 in. (45 cm) high

Front Leg

Seat is 12 in. (30 cm) high

Seat is 21 in. (53 cm) wide

TIP:
We have noted the important dimensions (but all the other sizes will depend on what pieces of wood you can find).

#adirondacklife

What You'll Need . . .

- Salvaged planks and sticks. The largest you need are 34 in. (87 cm) long and 6 in. (15 cm) wide. Other sizes are noted in the instructions below.
- Handsaw
- Tape measure and pencil
- Cordless drill/driver, bits and screws
- Sandpaper, leftover paint, and paintbrush

Your Adirondack chair will invite passive activities: daydreaming, snoozing, and reading.

2

Screw the back legs to the seat supports.

1. Cut two seat supports 30 in. (76 cm) long, 9 in. (23 cm) wide that tapers off to 7 in. (18 cm) at the front. Cut a 45° angle off the front ends and a 19° angle off the back ends as shown in the drawing. Bridge the seat supports with 21 in. (54 cm) long slats of varying widths (whatever is available) and screw them in place.

2. Cut two front leg support blocks 6 in. (15 cm) long from 2 x 2 in. (5 x 5 cm) sized wood and screw them to the seat supports 6 in. (15 cm) from the front. Cut two vertical supports for the back of the chair 14½ in. (37 cm) from 2 x 2 in. (5 x 5 cm) sized wood and screw them to the inside of the seat supports about 17 in. (43 cm) from the back.

3. Make the back from three boards 5–6 in. (12–15 cm) wide and 34 in. (87 cm) long. Cut angles off the tops of two of the boards as shown in the drawing on page 42. Arrange them in a flared shape, (also shown on page 42) but the exact shape is not critical. Join them using screws with one stick 10 in. (26 cm) from the top and another stick 21 in. (54 cm) set 5 in. (13 cm) from the bottom.

3

Screw the boards to the sticks.

4

Ask all your friends to help.

4. Make the frame as shown in the picture above. The front legs are 18½ in. (47 cm) long and 6 in. (15 cm) wide. The arms are 26 in. (66 cm) long and 9 in. (23 cm) wide. The arms and legs are spaced 21 in. (54 cm) apart and linked by 33 in. (84 cm) long horizontal rails at the front and back, screwed in place. The front legs are joined to the arms using support blocks and screws as shown in the diagram on page 42.

5. Rest the seat on the rail that links the two front legs, slide the back piece down between the arms and the seat, and screw the three parts together.

6. Smooth off any splinters and sharp edges using sandpaper, and then paint the whole chair in a color (or colors) of your choice.

TIP:

To prolong the life of Adirondack chairs, store indoors during the winter if possible. If storage space is not available, cover the chairs, first making sure they are completely dry to prevent mold.

Eco Food

The love of gardening
is a seed once sown
that never dies.

— Gertrude Jekyll, English garden designer and writer (1834–1932)

Herbs and Salad Greens

Have you ever grown your own salad? Growing your own food is one of those really amazing back-to-basics experiences that just shouldn't be missed. It's great fun—watching the plants develop, fighting off insects and bugs, harvesting—and then at the end of it all wolfing it down.

By planting easy-to-grow kitchen crops, you will understand the life cycles of annuals— food plants that die down every winter and start again from seed in the spring—and what they need to flourish. The herbs and greens you grow will give you the chance to practice your chef skills in the kitchen.

PLANT	SERVING IDEAS
Basil	pasta sauce, caprese (see page 84)
Spinach	salads, wraps
Lettuce	salads, sandwiches (see page 84)
Cilantro	tacos, salsa
Parsley	garnish
Oregano	pizza sauce

My garden
is my most
beautiful
masterpiece.

— Claude Monet , French
Impressionist painter (1840–1926)

Windowsill

This is a good idea if you don't have any outdoor space. You'll find that you can grow a surprising range of food crops on a windowsill. The easiest option is to go for fast-growing items like pick-and-eat salads, radishes, chives and herbs. You could find a ready-made window box, or make your own out of recycled materials, or you could just put up a shelf strong enough to take a row of recycled pots and tubs, or even some old buckets or paint cans.

Wall Planter

We built our planter with five short lengths of wood that we salvaged from a pallet, and an armful of split logs. We just screwed the planks together to make the box, and then fixed the logs with more screws.

Tomatoes

Home-grown tomatoes might be funny shapes and a bit small, but they taste simply wonderful. These days store-bought, non-organic tomatoes seem to be just big, tasteless bags of nothing, which is not really surprising because most aren't grown in soil or compost at all, but in chemical baths. For the real taste of tomatoes, you need to grow your own—then you'll know the difference!

Growing your own food and/or buying it in your local area also cuts down on packaging, transport costs, and pollution—a major step toward becoming an eco-warrior.

Tomatoes need pollination by insects such as bees, which you'll be able to observe happening firsthand if you plant them in a place you can visit often. By following the instructions on page 57 on how to make organic fertilizer, you'll understand how eco farmers solve the problem of feeding crops.

Why Is Organic Good?

Organic food is free from all the harmful chemicals that poison the land, wildlife, and us. Organic food might look a bit bumpy and lumpy, but it tastes, smells, and feels good.

The thankful receiver bears a plentiful harvest.

— William Blake , English Romantic poet and visual artist (1757–1827)

What You'll Need . . .

- A 2–3 in. (5–7.5 cm) deep seed-tray or found box
- Fine rich potting mix or the potting mix from tomato grow-bags
- Tomato seeds—an outdoor "bush" variety
- Sheet of clear plexiglass and some newspaper
- 12 x 3–5 in. (7.5–13 cm) pots or found containers
- Liquid tomato feed (see page opposite)
- Hanging basket or other container

1. Fill the seed-tray with the fine rich potting mix, remove any stones or bits and gently firm it level with your hands. Sprinkle the seeds over the potting mix, and cover them with a further thin layer of potting mix. Water with a fine spray, and cover the tray with a sheet of plexiglass topped with newspaper. Leave in a sheltered, sunny spot.

2. Two weeks or so after sowing the seeds, take the young seedlings one at a time from the tray and plant them in the 12 pots, filled with more potting mix.

3. Water the plants, give them a small liquid feed, and transfer them to a warm, sheltered spot.

4. When the plants are so big that they look as if they're going to jump out of their pots, carefully remove them and plant them into the much larger hanging pots or containers.

5. Finally, keep watering and feeding until the tomatoes look ready to be picked.

Liquid Feed for Tomatoes

Find a pair of old tights and stuff them full with fresh sheep or horse poo. Submerge it in a trash can full of water and leave to soak for 4–6 weeks. When your tomato plants start to bear fruit, give them increasingly bigger and bigger drinks of this liquid poo feed.

Poo is good for something!

FOOD PACKAGING: The Pros and Cons

Pros

✔ Reduces physical damage

✔ Makes it easier to transport

✔ Increases shelf life

Cons

✘ Increases transport costs

✘ Wasteful in raw materials

✘ Makes it difficult for us to inspect the food before buying

✘ Makes it difficult to present food that is in any way unusually big, small or bendy

✘ Increases waste

Low Tunnel for Crops

A low tunnel, also called solar tunnel, is like a one-man tent, but you grow plants in it. You can grow tomatoes or even orchids in the certain knowledge that they're going to be warm and protected from flies, birds, rabbits, and other pests.

3

Just as you and your pets need shelter, with this project, you will see how shelter helps plants, too. By working out how to construct this tunnel you will see how controlling temperature affects crop production—the greenhouse effect in action.

STEAM

A person who is growing
a garden, if he is growing
it organically, is improving
a piece of the world.

—Wendell Berry, American philosopher, writer, and farmer (1934–)

What You'll Need . . .

- 5 battens; 3 at 70 in. (180 cm) long and 2 at 47 in. (120 cm) long
- Handsaw
- Cordless drill/driver and bits
- Screws
- Blue plastic pipe; 2 pieces, 84 in. (214 cm) long
- 4 wooden pegs
- Clear plastic film

1. Screw four of the battens together to make a frame that's 70 in. (180 cm) long and 47 in. (120 cm) wide.

2. Reinforce the ends of the plastic pipe by banging wooden pegs into the ends. Screw through the tube ends and into the corners of the frame so you finish up with a tunnel shape.

3. Strengthen (brace) the tunnel with a batten fixed with screws that links the top curves.

4. Wrap the plastic film around the plastic tubes in one end of the tunnel and out the other until you have a complete tunnel. Seal the ends of the tunnel with short lengths of film (the film sticks to itself). Place your plants inside. Remove the tunnel for watering the plants.

Take Eco Action:
Write to Persuade Power

The best way to get someone in authority to listen to, consider, and act on your views is to write a letter to them. Your opinion really can change the world. We suggest sending your ideas, thoughts, and concerns about the environment to people "in power." This means your local council, government representatives, or the media. This template just reminds you of the important bits of information you need to include.

Your name and address,
telephone number,
and email address goes here

The person's full name,
their position in the organization,
and their address with zip code

Date

Title (think of a title or reference that describes
what your letter is about)

Dear Mr./Mrs. (add last name):

Write your letter here. It is very important to be polite; if
you're rude they will throw the letter away or contact you
and give you a good telling off!

Sign the letter here with your
usual signature

Print your full name clearly underneath

Runner Beans

You start with a few seeds and very soon you've got plenty of lush green beans. It's an adventure—thinking about the variety to grow, watching the plants develop, building a support "teepee," fighting off harmful insects and bugs, harvesting, and then at the end of it all having plate after plate piled high with beautiful, tasty runner beans.

The fun is in designing a sturdy structure for the beans to climb up and then, after watering your plants well, watching the "hanging garden" take over the structure. Along the way you will learn to identify which pests pose a problem for your crop, and how to manage them.

What You'll Need . . .

- Scrap length of blue plastic pipe long enough to make a hoop to fit the bag and a 5 in. (13 cm) length of "broomstick" dowel.
- Handsaw
- Dumpy bag—the sort of bag used by contractors
- Wooden pallet
- Spent mushroom compost
- Pot-grown runner-bean seedlings
- 8 strong sticks made from a wood species like beech and a ball of strong string

Push the two ends so that they come together on the wooden "broomstick" dowel.

Fold the edges of the bulging bag down over the hoop.

1. Cut the plastic tube to length so that it makes a hoop that is a tight fit in the neck of the bag. Bang the length of "broomstick" dowel into one end of the tube and use it to join the two ends together to make a hoop.

2. Sit the dumpy bag on the pallet, and start to fill it with the compost/soil mix. When the bag is about half full, put the hoop over the outside of the bag and fold the top of the bag over on itself so that the hoop is covered. Add more compost/soil mix until the bag starts to bulge and the hoop is held in place.

More Ways to Grow Runner Beans

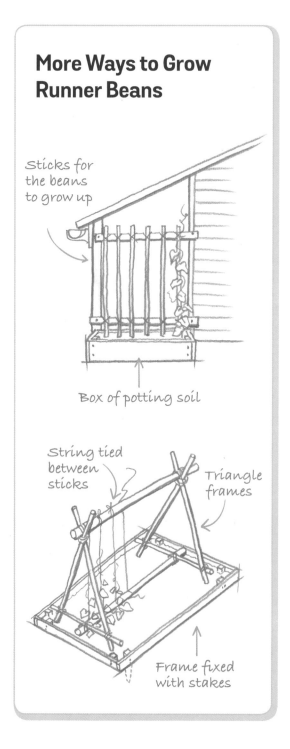

Sticks for the beans to grow up

Box of potting soil

String tied between sticks

Triangle frames

Frame fixed with stakes

3

Plant the seedlings about 9–12 in. (23–30 cm) apart.

3. Stamp the compost/soil mix down until it's firm. Plant the seedlings in 3 in. (8 cm) deep holes in the compost about 9–12 in. (23–30 cm) apart. Water well.

4. Once the plants start to grow strongly, put the sticks around the bag to make a "teepee" frame for the beans to grow around. Make sure you sink the sticks well into the ground and tie the sticks together at the top with strong string.

TIP:
The teepee
must be sturdy.

Potatoes

Have you ever eaten your own spuds? Growing your own potatoes is really exciting. You put in a dozen wrinkly old "seed potatoes," and these turn into bucketfuls of smooth, shiny, tasty spuds. Of course digging them up is good fun, a bit like hunting for buried treasure, but best of all is eating them.

4

Digging up your new spuds is cool!

With a bit of extra work to fashion a container sturdy enough to house a potato crop, you'll learn how tuber crops, crops that grow from fleshy underground stems, create new plants in a way similar but not identical to seed plants.

For me, a plain baked potato
is the most delicious one. . . .
It is soothing and enough.

—M.F.K. Fisher, American food writer (1908—1992)

What You'll Need . . .

- Scrap length of blue plastic pipe long enough to make a hoop to fit the bag and a 5 in. (13 cm) length of "broomstick" dowel
- Dumpy bag
- Wooden pallet
- Spent mushroom compost
- 4 iron hook-ended fence stakes
- Strong plastic rope, 26 ft. (8 m) long
- Large darning needle and some thin nylon string
- Sprouting seed potatoes

1. Prepare the dumpy bag as in steps 1 and 2 of the bean project (see page 65).

2. Push the iron fence stakes into the ground— one at each "corner" of the bag. Use rope to tie the bag loops to the top of the stakes. Use the needle and nylon string to sew the edge over the hoop.

3. Plant the seed potatoes so that they are about 9–12 in. (23–30 cm) apart and 3–6 in. (7.5–15 cm) deep and then just sit back and wait for them to grow.

4. When the leaves and flowers fade, the new potatoes are ready to be dug up (see page 68). To cook them, first wash off all the dirt, and boil them for 20–30 minutes. You can then pile them high up on your plate, dribble them with butter or olive oil, cover them with baked beans, and start eating.

2

Sew the rolled-over edge of the bag to the hoop

3

Chicken: Free Range vs. Factory Farm

A "battery chicken" or hen spends all its life in a small wire cage, standing on crippled legs and feet on a space no bigger than a sheet of typing paper. Battery-bred chicken meat is cheap because the system keeps costs down by treating the hen as a product, like baked beans. If the hen is ill or doesn't lay, it is killed.

Meanwhile, a truly free-range chicken is free to roam and live its life in a field—it can run, flap, peck, eat insects, and generally do what chickens enjoy doing. Turn the page for a project that will let you experience the joy of having happy chickens—and their eggs!

Backyard Chicken Coop

Chickens don't just lay eggs—they are also great fun to watch! They chase and fight each other for tasty snacks like worms, flies, beetles and bugs, save time by peeing and pooing from the same hole, and enjoy nothing more than "bathing" in dusty holes in the ground. After a hard day's work they perch precariously on a stick or tree branch and go to sleep.

The best way of getting a really good egg—fresh, tasty, and free from additives—is to keep your own chickens. Even better, when you're feeding your kitchen scraps to the chickens and eating your own eggs rather than store-bought ones, you're cutting down on food waste and all the packaging and transport that is needed for store-bought goods. Keeping chickens is an all around eco winner!

Unique in this book, this project gives you the chance to try your hand at animal agriculture—right in your backyard! If you live in the city, first be sure to have a grownup check the local rules on keeping chickens for you. Constructing the coop will give you a fun problem-solving challenge: how to keep the chickens in, and happy, while keeping other animals out.

What You'll Need . . .

- A good supply of salvaged wood
- Handsaw
- Tape measure
- Try-square
- Cordless drill/driver and bits
- Hammer, nails, screws, string, and fencing staples
- Six hinges and two bolts (locking mechanisms)
- Chicken wire

1. Our chicken coop is 84 in. (214 cm) long, 36 in. (92 cm) wide and 48 in. (122 cm) high and suitable for two chickens. It is made from odds and ends of salvaged wood. The construction and size of your chicken coop will depend on how many chickens you have and the sizes of your bits of wood. The following steps give general information about our chicken coop that you can use as a guide for building your own.

2. The nesting box part measures 30 in. (76 cm) wide, 36 in. (92 cm) deep and 24 in. (61 cm) high with a similar size covered area below. Use a handsaw to cut the plywood or tongue-and-groove wood to size so that you have a roof panel at 36 x 30 in. (92 cm x 76 cm), a base panel at 36 x 30 in. (92 cm x 76 cm), a back panel 24 x 30 in. (61 x 76 cm) and two side panels each at 36 x 24 in. (92 x 61 cm). Join these panels to each other using battens and screws on the inside corners to make an open fronted box that stands on 24 in. (61 cm)-long legs. Set the roof at a sloping angle by the addition of a plank of wood at the front about 6 in. (15 cm) wide.

3. Clad the area under the nesting box with wood screwed to the legs but leave the side facing into the cage open.

4. Cover the triangular ventilation holes each side of the roof with chicken wire stapled in place.

5. Make a door to fit the front of the nesting box and fix it in place with two hinges and a bolt or catch.

6. Inside the nesting box is a horizontal stick, 9 in. (23 cm) off the floor and 6 in. (15 cm) from the back for the chickens to perch on and sleep at night. Fix this with screws.

7. Cut a door hole approximately 24 in. (61 cm) high and 9 in. (23 cm) wide in the side of the nesting box that faces into the cage. Cut a door to fit the doorway and hinge it at the bottom (so that when opened it forms a ramp).

OK . . . so who is the chicken now?

8. To build the run use the battens to make 4 identical frames about 24 in. (61 cm) wide and 48 in. (122 cm) high. Join and reinforce the corners with little triangular blocks of wood and screws.

9. Take the four frames, screw them together in pairs, and fit them to the side of the nesting box.

10. Make a frame 48 in. (122 cm) high and 36 in. (92 cm) wide from battens, corner blocks and screws. Fix it to the end of the run with screws. For the door at the end of the run make another identical frame and fix it with hinges and a bolt or catch.

11. Cut a 3 ft. batten and screw it inside the cage to make a horizontal support for the nesting box door to rest on when open. Now cut and fix a ramp to one side of the nesting box door, that runs from the horizontal support down to the end of the cage.

DID YOU KNOW?

A hen that lays one egg every day is a very good layer.

12. Cut, fit, and staple chicken wire to the sides, top and door of the run. Add extra battens to reinforce the nesting box, run and doors wherever you think the structure needs to be strengthened. Screw or nail these in place.

13. Two horizontal sticks 90 in. (229 cm) long reinforce the structure and form handles for dragging the house to new locations.

14. Attach string to the top of the nesting box door (inside the run) and run it through holes in and out of the nesting box so you can open and close the door from outside.

15. Spread wood shavings on the floor of the nesting box, provide food and water in the run, and introduce your chickens to their new home.

Make sure to bang *the* nail, not *your* nail—that would hurt quite a lot.

More Coop Construction Ideas

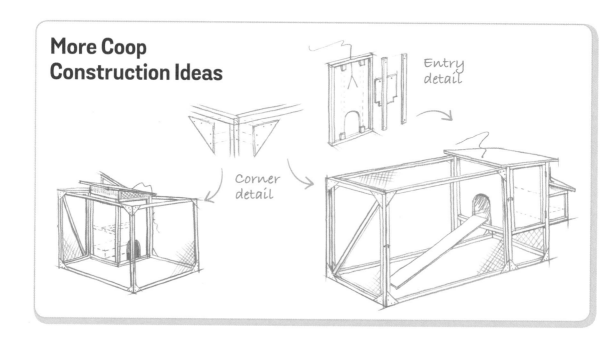

Can You Make a Chicken Coop from Recycled Materials?

You can make a chicken coop from just about any mix of materials that will keep the chickens warm and dry in the winter, and cool and fresh in the summer. We made ours from bits of plywood, waterproof plastic, battens, and such like—materials left over from making the eco den (see pages 18–31). You could make yours from an old shed, a wooden packing case, a frame covered in roof felt and tin—in fact anything you can knock together to make a little hut.

Are Chickens Easy to Keep?

If you give your chickens a dry and airy house, and provide them with plenty of food and fresh water, then they are relatively easy to keep. The best advice, before you get your own chickens, is to talk to any friends and neighbors who keep chickens, visit your vet, talk to local "chicken-fancier" groups, and generally do your homework until you know all the do's and don'ts of chicken-keeping.

TIP:
Turn to page 85 for four delicious ways to cook your fresh eggs!

How Many Eggs Will You Get?

Two healthy, well-looked-after chickens will give you anything from 6 to 14 eggs a week, all depending upon their breed, their age, the weather, and the time of year. When everything is just right, a pair of hens will give you about 600 eggs a year—say 12 eggs a week. If the chickens get ill, or if you occasionally miss out on giving them their food and/or water, for whatever reason, then you can expect them to produce fewer eggs. Collecting and eating your first fresh egg will be an experience you'll never forget!

Butter

At school we were given a bottle of milk to drink during our break. Sometimes we would shake our bottles until the cream turned to butter! We would then give the warm and sticky leftover part of the milk to the school cat, and save the blob of butter to spread on our lunchtime sandwiches.

What You'll Need . . .

- Hand-sized jam-jar with screw-top lid
- Enough full-cream milk to fill the jar
- Fine-weave cotton cloth

- 2 Bowls
- Small pinch of salt

With this project you'll learn the old-fashioned science of rustic food processing . . . and give your arm a workout, too! Butter is created when fat molecules separate out of the thick milk solution, or mixture in which a solid disappears into a liquid, and clump together. How much you shake and the temperature of the milk both affect how long the process takes.

1. Sit in the sun with your screw-top jar full of rich, creamy milk and shake it up and down for about an hour, until the creamy part of the milk has formed into a little ball.

2. Unscrew the lid and use the cloth and one bowl to strain off the liquid (called "whey"). Mix the salt into the butter in a separate bowl and put it in the fridge.

1

2

Straining.

Foraged Berry Milkshake

Be warned—some berries are poisonous! You must check with an adult before eating any wild berry. Blackberries and strawberries are easy to identify and packed full of flavor. They're also eco-stars on every count—they're completely organic, they're free if you take the trouble to go out and collect them, and they don't involve any packaging or transport to stores.

The very best berries are always found out in the wilds, in quiet areas, away from roads, where not many people go. To put it another way, you don't want to be eating berries if there's a chance that they could have been blasted with polluting car-exhaust fumes, sprayed with weed killer, sloshed with cow patties, or dribbled with dog pee.

What's most important for this project is the correct identification of edible wild berry species. You'll practice being the neighborhood naturalist—and end up with a delicious brain-recharging snack full of vitamins and antioxidants, or substances that protect your cells from damage. Any nutritionist, or person who studies the health benefits of foods, will tell you this shake is a great treat!

Better than any argument
is to rise at dawn and pick
dew-wet red berries in a cup.

— Wendell Berry , American philosopher,
writer, and farmer (1934–)

What You'll Need . . .

- 3 handfuls of wild blackberries
- 2 large bowls
- Potato masher
- Open-textured cloth (such as muslin)
- Wooden spoon
- Crushed ice
- Glass of milk

1. Get all your blackberries checked over by a trusted adult—just to make sure you haven't picked anything that might be poisonous.

2. Remove anything that wriggles, squiggles, slithers or hops—things like flies, maggots, worms, caterpillars, and bugs. Pick off any stalks or spiky bits, and throw away anything that looks dry, moldy or in any way bad.

1

3

3. Wash the blackberries under running water, put them in one of the bowls (save a few for decorating), and squash them with the masher until they're nicely pulped.

4. Pour the pulp into the cloth over the other bowl. Gently press the pulp with the wooden spoon until all the juice and some of the thick bits have gone through the cloth into the bowl.

5. Add the milk to the berry juice, mix it together, put in the fridge until it's cold, decorate with more berries and it's ready!

5

Mealtime!

Use a mezzaluna to chop herbs so that you can't cut your hand.

Combine fresh basil and fresh tomato with pepper, olive oil, and mozzarella cheese for a mouthwatering caprese (sounds like kah-pray-zay) salad.

TIP:
It's best to grow or raise your own food, but if that's not an option the next best thing is to buy from local organic farmers or farmers markets.

Giant salad sandwiches are good for you!

How to Cook Eggs . . .

Boiled

Put two eggs in a saucepan, cover them with water and boil for five minutes. Carefully remove the eggs and slice their tops off with a knife. Use a spoon to eat the eggs, with some bread and butter.

Scrambled

Dribble a small dash of olive oil into a saucepan and put it on the heat. Whisk the eggs with a small amount of milk and pour into the pan. Keep stirring the egg with a fork until it's just cooked. Spoon the cooked egg out onto a slice of toast, sprinkle (if you like) with salt and black pepper, and eat straight away.

Poached

Put some water into a saucepan, pour in a splash of vinegar, and put it on the heat. Break the eggs one at a time into the gently boiling water. Cook until the egg white goes solid. Spoon the eggs out, drain them carefully, place them on a slice of warm toast, and eat with your fingers. (If you like it, spread the toast first with some yeast extract.)

Fried

Dribble olive oil into a frying pan and heat it until it sizzles. Break the eggs one at a time into the pan. Leave the yolks whole or break them with a spatula—the choice is yours. Use the spatula to flip the egg over, wait until the edges are crisp and turn it out onto a fat slice of brown bread.

Take Eco Action:
Buy Eco-Friendly Food

DID YOU KNOW?

Even though pesticides are sprayed on land, many times, they can make their way into a water source, such as a river, ocean, or pond. If a body of water becomes contaminated with the chemicals, many fish and other animals may die and get sick. This can throw the whole ecosystem off balance.

Crop dusting (spraying chemicals on plants).

Chemical Farming and Subsidies

Chemicals increase crop yields (meaning how much is produced), and government money in the form of farm subsidies keeps farmers happy, but both result in low-quality, low-priced food. Do you think this is a good idea?

"Milk Quotas" and "Butter Mountains"

Milk quotas—limits on how much milk each farmer could sell—were a government means of controlling milk production. This resulted in mountains of butter (made from the milk that couldn't be sold), imbalances in supply and costs, and low animal-welfare standards.

How Does World Trade Affect You and the Environment?

World trade affects everything from the environment and the well-being of farmers all over the world to your own health. Your liking for, say, lots of low-cost chocolate, and my liking for a cup of low-cost coffee, might mean that some poor farmers in somewhere like South America or Africa have to miss out on a square meal because they can't get a fair price for their produce. This may lead to lower-quality chocolate and coffee.

Eco Energy
and Water

The first law of ecology is that everything is related to everything else.

— Barry Commoner, American cellular biologist and environmentalist (1917–2012)

Wind Turbine

You can build a wind turbine that will power a small light for your den or shed. If your outdoor space is limited, make a smaller version and consider attaching it to the top of the den or shed.

Most wind turbines have anything from two to five blades, a bit like an old-fashioned airplane. Wind pushes on the blades, which forces them to move around. The spinning "hub" in the center then generates electricity.

What Are the Advantages of a Wind Turbine?

ADVANTAGES 😊	DISADVANTAGES 🙁
Wind is free!	Wind turbines only work when the wind blows!
Wind turbines don't produce CO_2 or radioactive waste like power stations do.	Some people think that wind turbines look ugly and are noisy.
Wind turbines have a small "physical footprint" (the amount of ground they take up) so the surrounding land can still be used for farming.	Some people think that the whirling blades kill birds.
Small wind turbines can be erected at people's homes to generate off-grid energy. (see page 29)	If it takes one giant turbine to power 5,000 homes, a city like London would need at least 6,000 turbines— but where could they be built?

Using a repurposed bicycle dynamo, LED light, found items, and some elbow grease, you'll learn the basic technology of wind turbine electricity generation—a major source of renewable energy, especially in Europe. Get to know how wind works and you'll know your wind turbine's abilities and limitations well. In addition, your hand-built wind turbine will dazzle all your friends!

What You'll Need . . .

- DIY tools, including jigsaw, handsaw, cordless drill/driver and bits, and hammer
- 2 pieces of PVC pipe, 4 in. (10 cm) in diameter and 24 in. (60 cm) long
- Pair of compasses
- 2 pieces of exterior plywood about 12 in. (30 cm) square
- Ruler and pencil
- 6V bicycle hub dynamo—we found ours in a dumpster but you can buy locally or online
- Screws, nuts, bolts, washers, plastic ties, and jubilee clip (sizes to suit your found materials)

- U-shaped metal bracket for fixing the hub to the mast—ours came from an old gate
- Found item for the "tail"—we used an old fish-barbecue grill and a sheet of plastic, but you could use an old tennis racket and the plastic
- 164 ft. (50 m) 6V 2-core electric cable
- Electrical amalgamating tape
- 15 ft. (4.5 m) long metal pipe for the mast—we used 2 old pieces joined together
- Rope and tensioning cleats
- 6V solar LED shed light kit

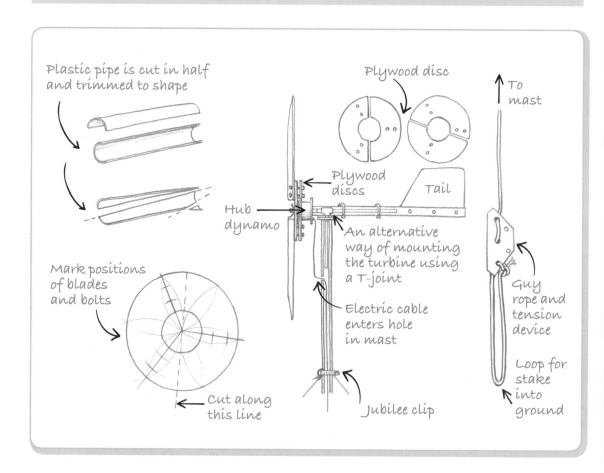

Plastic pipe is cut in half and trimmed to shape

Plywood disc

To mast

Plywood discs

Tail

Hub dynamo

An alternative way of mounting the turbine using a T-joint

Electric cable enters hole in mast

Mark positions of blades and bolts

Cut along this line

Jubilee clip

Guy rope and tension device

Loop for stake into ground

1. Decide where you want the turbine to stand. It needs to be as near the light as possible and nowhere near overhead wires, buildings, or neighbors. Check with an adult before you start.

2. Saw each of the two pieces of pipe in half lengthways so that you finish up with four turbine blades (keep one for spare). Trim the blades to the finished shape (see drawing).

3. Use the compasses to mark two circles of plywood about three times larger in diameter than the hub dynamo. Cut out the discs.

4. On both discs, draw a circle in the center that's the same size as the hub. Set the compasses to the radius of the plywood disc, spike the point anywhere on the circumference, and draw an arc right through the circle. Reposition the point of the compasses to where the arc intersects the circumference (you can use either intersection) and draw another arc as before. Repeat this procedure around the circumference until you have six "petal" shapes (see drawing far left). Use a ruler and pencil to mark straight lines from the center of the disc to the circumference through the center of every other petal. Move the compass's point to the center of the disc and mark bolt holes on the petal center lines in roughly the positions indicated in the diagram (not critical). Mark a cut line between two petals. Then cut each disc in half and cut out the center holes with a jigsaw (an adult will need to do this for you).

5. Fit the half–discs around the hub; ensure that the cut lines offset. Screw them to each other at regular intervals. Drill holes through the blades and plywood discs at the points already marked, and fix the blades in position using bolts, nuts, and washers. Reinforce the discs with additional bolts as shown at right.

Making the blades.

Reinforce the discs with extra bolts.

6

Hub bracket, tail fixing and cable connection (steps 6–8).

9

Fitting to the mast (steps 9–10).

6. Bolt a U-shaped metal bracket to the back of the hub. Drill holes in the ends of the bracket that are large enough to take your mast (make it a loose fit so that the turbine can rotate as the wind changes direction). If you can't find a bracket, make one from scrap metal.

7. Fix the tail vane to the bracket by binding it with coat-hanger wire or clamping it with jubilee clips.

8. Connect the cable to the screws in the electrical contacts on the dynamo (fit one core to each contact) and bind with amalgamating tape. Ask an adult to help.

9. Fix the turbine on top of the mast using a washer and a jubilee clip above and below the U-shaped bracket. The fixing order is fit a jubilee clip about 6 in. (15 cm) down the mast, slide a washer down the mast so it rests on the jubilee clip, slide the U-shaped bracket on the mast so it's resting on the washer, slide a washer so it rests on the top of the bracket, and finish with a jubilee clip.

10. Dig a 12 in. (30 cm) deep hole in the ground and put a brick or similar in the bottom of the hole for the mast to rest on. Tie four strong guy ropes to the mast and add tension devices as shown in the diagram on page 92.

11. Connect the electric cable to the solar LED light kit. If you like, you can run it down through the mast by making a hole at the top and another at the bottom. Then just wait for the wind to blow!

What Makes the Wind Blow?

If you open a window in your house in winter, you'll feel cold air rushing in. The same thing happens on a larger scale around our planet. The earth's air or atmosphere is heated by the sun, but this doesn't happen evenly. Winds are created when areas of hot air (less dense) and cold air (more dense) move and mix in an effort to even out temperature differences.

DID YOU KNOW?

Many of the biggest wind turbines in the world have been built in Germany. One near the village of Gaildorf, for example, is 584 ft. (178 m) high (23 times the height of a house) and can provide enough power for thousands of homes.

Photovoltaic Cells

A photovoltaic (PV) cell, or solar panel, converts sunlight into electricity. It will make "direct current" (DC) electricity, which is like that produced by a battery. Each PV cell contains a back contact, two silicon layers, an anti-reflective coating, and a contact grid.

Things called "photons" in sunlight are absorbed and passed through the material within the solar panel. The photons agitate particles called "electrons" in this material, and the movement of these electrons creates electricity. To put it more simply, sunlight goes in one end and electricity comes out the other.

A low-cost PV cell will easily power a few LED lights, a cellphone charger, a laptop computer, a small radio—in fact, almost any small electrical item that is normally powered by batteries. Just in case you or your parents are worried, a low-voltage item of this type is safe to handle. A solar-powered shed-lighting kit is a typical low-cost example, and is very easy to set up—consider adding one to your shed!

Like wind power, solar power is completely sustainable and an increasingly important source of energy for human civilization. All you need is the right technology to capture it, and by experimenting with solar panels you will gain firsthand knowledge about how sunshine can be turned into useful electricity—pollution free.

TIP:
Experiment and see what happens!

Solar-Powered Buggy

Would you like to play with a solar-powered "moon buggy?" You can buy all sorts of kits for making something along these lines, but our buggy is extra special on at least two counts: it can be made from easily found basic materials, and all the workings are on view.

It's really simple—the top-mounted solar panel powers the motor, the motor drives the rear axle, and the rear axle turns the back wheels. Best of all, though, the design is flexible enough to allow for a whole range of modifications.

The good eco bit about this machine is that almost everything on it can be made either from things like plastic cotton reels, foam tubes, and cardboard, or from items scavenged from other toys. You have two options: you can settle for building the basic form and leave it at that, or you can build the basic form and then make modifications. For example, you could dramatically increase the size of the solar panel and motor and make a larger vehicle, you could have a motor for each wheel, you could design a much fancier body, you could use the model as a prototype for a large go-kart-type buggy that a person could actually sit on—there are lots of exciting possibilities, so let your imagination run wild.

Turn solar energy into motion by building a very basic car from scratch. Once you have the fundamentals of the solar technology and materials down, and a good grasp of automotive engineering, there's no end to the possibilities of how you can make your car or buggy look.

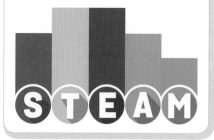

What You'll Need . . .

- About 30 in. (75 cm) of ⅜ in. (9 mm) square-section wood
- Handsaw
- Household items such as scraps of wood, stiff cardboard, masking tape, PVA glue, battery-type cables and switches, hole punch, scissors, and a strong elastic band
- 2 x 8 in. (20 cm) lengths of ³⁄₁₆ in. (4.5 mm) diameter wooden dowel

- 4 cotton reels and 1 slightly smaller cotton reel
- About 6 in. (15 cm) of foam tubing, large enough to be a tight sleeve-like fit on the cotton reels
- Plastic "sleeve"
- Small, low-voltage, battery-driven, model makers' motor
- Photovoltaic solar panel—large enough to drive the motor

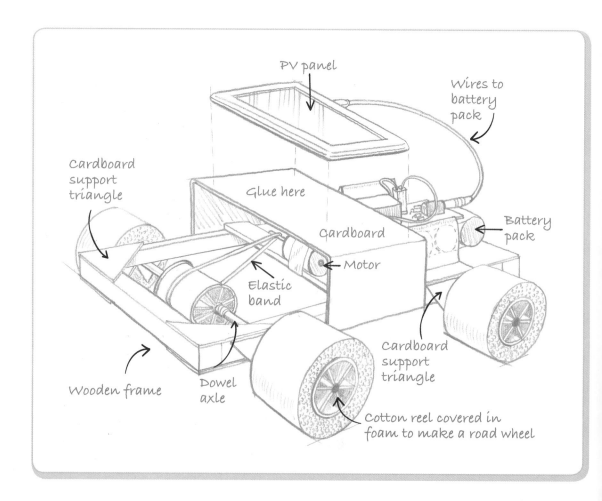

PV panel

Wires to battery pack

Cardboard support triangle

Glue here

Cardboard

Battery pack

Motor

Elastic band

Wooden frame

Dowel axle

Cardboard support triangle

Cotton reel covered in foam to make a road wheel

1. Have a scavenge to see what you can come up with. Things like the cotton reels are common enough, so it's only when you come to the electrics that you might have difficulties. Items like the motor and the fine wire cables can usually be found on and in broken flashlights, radios, and remote-controlled cars.

2. When you've found all the bits, start by cutting the 30 in. (75 cm) section of wood into four lengths using a handsaw—you need two about 9 in. (23 cm) long and two about 5 in. (13 cm) long.

3. Glue the wood together so that you have a chassis frame about 10 in. (25 cm) long and 5 in. (13 cm) wide. Strengthen the corners of the frame with small triangles of stiff cardboard.

4. Cut out four more little triangle shapes for the axle supports, punch holes to take the axles, and be ready to stick them in place on either side of the chassis frame.

5. Stick the two front axle supports to the chassis, run the front dowel through its axle supports, bind the ends with the masking tape—until they are a nice tight push-fit for the cotton reels—and then push the cotton reels into place.

6. For the back axle, repeat the masking tape binding bit as in step 5, only this time you need to have three bindings, one each for the road wheels and one for the drive wheel in the center. Fit the drive wheel, position the elastic band as shown, stick on the axle support triangles, and then fit the two road wheels.

7. Cut the foam tubing to make tires and slide them in place over the cotton-reel wheels.

8. Cut, fit, and glue the motor mounting board in place across the chassis.

9. Fit a found plastic sleeve on the shaft of the motor, cut a V-slot in the sleeve (for the elastic band), and use the masking tape to strap the motor to the mounting board.

10. Cut a length of cardboard to support the PV panel and glue the ends to the sides of the chassis so that the solar panel is looking to the sky. Glue the solar panel onto the cardboard.

11. Fit the cables to the solar panel and the motor, stand the buggy in the sun, and just see what happens (it will move by itself but you cannot steer it).

12. Finally, when everything is up and running and you have made any necessary adjustments to the basic machine, you can start thinking about how you're going to decorate your buggy.

Different Ways of Capturing Heat from the Sun

- **Flat collectors**—an array of metal pipes or glass tubes through which water is passed. The sun shines on the tubes and heats the water. The resulting hot water goes to a storage tank.

- **Wide-angle collectors**—an array of metal tubes set together with a curved metal reflector. The curved metal concentrates the heat from the sun. These are also used to heat water.

- **Evacuated tubes**—an array of glass tubes that have mirror-like surfaces to concentrate the sun's rays. The sun heats a pointed copper lump that in turn heats water.

- **Trombe wall**—a hollow brick or concrete wall-like structure usually found in a conservatory. The sun heats the wall from the outside during the day, and the wall gives off heat to the inside during the night.

The Sun—
What Is It?

The sun is about 840,000 miles (1.35 million km) in diameter (100 times greater than that of the Earth), and made up mainly of hot gases. The temperature at its center is at least 10 million kelvins. The surface, however, is only 5,800 kelvins—say 20 times hotter than a cup of tea!

Solar-Heated Pool

This paddling pool uses the power of the sun to heat up the water. Here you can make your very own "concentrating solar thermal device"—this sounds fancy but just means something that creates heat by using the sun. It's a version of flat collector (see page 102), with the pool acting as the "storage tank."

When the pool is full of cold water, you operate a hand pump to move some of the water up to the top of the slope. The water then dribbles out of holes in the pipe and falls onto a sunbaked corrugated-metal sheet. As it runs down the channels in this "chute," the water heats up, and the pool is filled with warm water.

Using solar energy to heat water means that swimming time can be extended, though not at night. You'll get accustomed to using basic pump technology to move water, and will understand how flat collector systems (see page 102) help people take their showers off-grid. You'll get a sense of why water is an important medium for heating and cooling systems, too.

What You'll Need . . .

- Plenty of straw, plus 2 extra bales
- Lots of rope and string
- Large plastic sheet 142 x 142 in. (360 x 360 cm)
- Sheet of corrugated metal, 94 in. (240 cm) long and 35 in. (90 cm) wide
- 7 wooden battens, 59 in. (150 cm) long
- Plastic guttering, 2 pieces at least 40 in. (100 cm) long
- Hand pump—we used a wartime fire pump but you could use a low-cost bilge pump available from a boat shop
- 142 in. (360 cm) length of hose
- Old plastic water tank or some other container (optional)
- Household and garden tools such as tape measure, level, and handsaw

1. Decide on the size of your pool and form the straw into a sausage shape long enough to form the circumference. Bind the sausage up with rope or string so that you have a big fat hoop like a giant doughnut. Look at the drawings and see how the inner diameter and fatness of the hoop decide the size and depth of the pool.

2. Drape the plastic sheet over the sausage hoop and use a hose to fill the central space up slowly with water.

3. When the water starts to brim over, wrap the rope around the outside of the whole thing and knot it off securely.

4. Lay the corrugated sheet on the ground, and bang battens into the ground 6 in. (15 cm) along from each corner. Saw off the tops of the battens so that the two nearest the pool are 24 in. (61 cm) high and the others are 47

in. (120 cm). Link the shorter battens with a horizontal batten at the top, held in place with rope or string. Place two straw bales one on top of the other, between the other pair of battens. Add a horizontal batten on top of the bales and then another batten to the top ends of the vertical battens. Rest (not fix) the corrugated sheet on the battens. Add on guttering to the lower end of the corrugated sheet and another length linking the first piece of gutter to the pool.

5. Fit to your hand pump a hose that runs from the pool up to the top of the metal slope.

6. You now have a choice: either attach the top end of the hose to the top of the slope and make holes in the hose so that there is a well-placed dribble point above each of the channels in the corrugated sheet; or run the hose into a holding tank that, in turn, dribbles water through carefully placed holes.

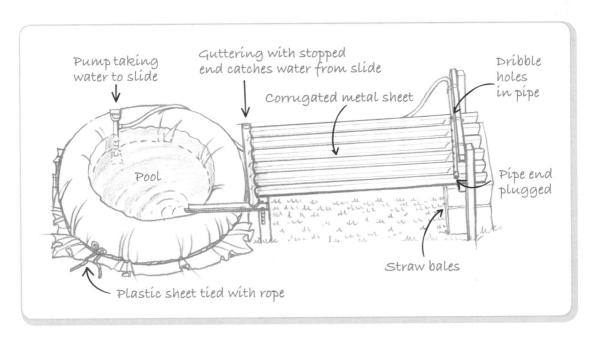

Pump taking water to slide

Guttering with stopped end catches water from slide

Corrugated metal sheet

Dribble holes in pipe

Pool

Pipe end plugged

Straw bales

Plastic sheet tied with rope

Rain Barrel

Water is all around us, in lakes, rivers, and the sea, but purifying and pumping it takes power (producing harmful carbon dioxide). Here is a way to collect and filter water and save on that power. The filtered water can be used for washing, washing-up, or boiling (DO NOT drink it without boiling it first) and any wastewater from the sink is drained into a bucket and used for watering plants.

Water is the driving force of all nature.

— Leonardo da Vinci, Italian Renaissance painter, architect, and scientist (1452–1519)

Most of us take a plentiful supply of clean water for granted. By constructing your own water filtering system that collects, cleans, and stores rainwater, you'll have the chance to learn basic water chemistry as well as practice water sustainability.

What You'll Need . . .

- Six wheelbarrow loads of bricks and slabs
- Large sink
- 2 water barrels with taps
- 40 in. (100 cm) plastic pipe, 40 in. (100 cm) guttering and tank connectors
- Drill with a bit of the same diameter as the plastic pipe

- 79 in. (200 cm) long wooden batten
- Handsaw
- Tape measure
- Bucket
- 1 bag each of pea gravel, barbecue charcoal, and sand

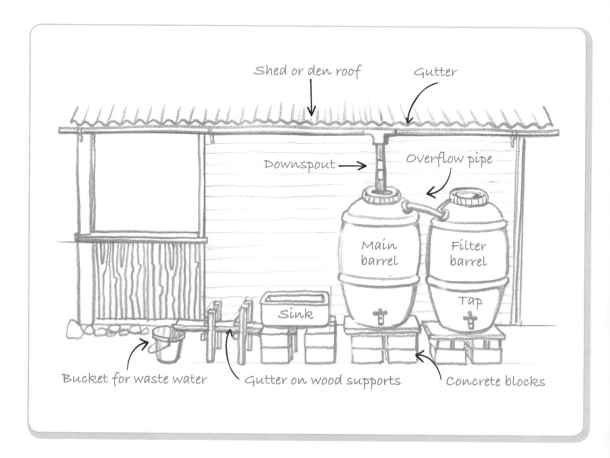

Shed or den roof

Gutter

Downspout →

Overflow pipe

Main barrel

Filter barrel

Tap

Sink

Bucket for waste water

Gutter on wood supports

Concrete blocks

1. Arrange the bricks and slabs so that you have platforms that can support the sink and the two water barrels (one barrel should be at a slightly higher level so that the water can run downhill from one to the other). The heights of the platforms should allow room for a bucket to sit below the tap in the filter barrel, and for water to run from the sink along a gutter pipe into a waste bucket. Install the two barrels and sink, and connect the main barrel to the gutter with a downspout.

2. Mark the position of the overflow pipe on the main barrel and the inflow pipe on the filter barrel. Drill holes and link the two barrels with a short length of pipe.

3. Use odds and ends of batten and plastic guttering to make a channel running from the underside of the sink and down toward the waste bucket (which might need to be set in a hole in the ground).

4. Fill the filter barrel with the layers of filter material—gravel, charcoal, and sand—as shown in the diagram below.

5. If you like, you can paint the barrels in your favorite colors to jazz them up a bit.

Cross-Section of the Filter System

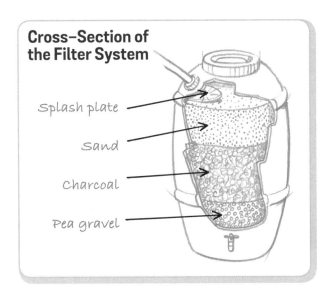

Splash plate

Sand

Charcoal

Pea gravel

SHORTER SHOWERS

In many countries, people take a bath or a shower every day, leave taps running, and use automatic washing machines. This means that we each get through around 30 buckets of water a day. If you use about 50 gallons (about 225 liters) of water for a 10-minute shower, and you live for 80 years, then 50 x 365 = 18,250 gallons (225 x 365 = 82,125 liters) in a year x 80 = about 1.5 million gallons (about 6.5 million liters) in your lifetime! Is it time to start taking fewer, shorter showers?

Take Eco Action:
Acknowledge Challenges

Hurricanes, Wildfires, and Floods

According to the US government, human-caused global warming will result in longer droughts, heavier rainfall, worse floods, hotter heat waves, and bigger hurricanes. The report says that extreme weather events will be more commonplace and more intense. It's probably a good idea to talk about this with your teachers and parents to see what they think.

San Juan, Puerto Rico after 2017's Hurricane Maria.

What Is the Kyoto Protocol? And the Paris Agreement?

The Kyoto Protocol is a set of rules, decided by 137 countries, relating to discussions on climate change. The idea is that the rules will be used as a guide when the countries come to talk about such matters as greenhouse gas emissions. Although these countries have been talking since 1997, they haven't yet agreed on what they have agreed. How's that for complicated?

Fifteen of the 20 biggest wildfires in California history have happened since 2000.

Population Boom

The world's population is growing fast—in the year 1800 it was about 900 million, in 1900 it was about 1.6 billion, in 2010 it was about 6.9 billion, and it's still rising. How many people do you think there'll be in the year 2100?

Times Square, New York.

Livestock Emissions

Livestock, meaning animals like sheep and cows, fart so much that they produce more greenhouse gas than cars. With the earth's population growing and with more meat being so cheap (see page 71), the global consumption of meat is going up rather than down. Should people eat less meat?

Cattle penned inside a Concentrated Animal Feeding Operation, or CAFO, in New Mexico.

Weather Station

This is a place where you can make observations about the weather and record your findings. It has various instruments and pieces of equipment that will help you monitor the weather and make your own forecasts or predictions.

Designed by the father of Robert Louis Stevenson (the author who wrote *Treasure Island*), the weatherproof box (called a "Stevenson Screen") is a cabinet for weather-recording instruments. The white, ventilated structure keeps the recording equipment both dry and shaded. In addition to the cabinet, a proper weather station is made up by a notebook for keeping records, a "minimum and maximum" thermometer to show the lowest and highest temperatures, a barometer to show air pressure, a hygrometer to show humidity (amount of moisture in the air), a rain gauge to show rainfall amounts, a weather/wind vane to show the wind direction, an anemometer to record the wind speed, and a compass so that you know which way the weather is moving.

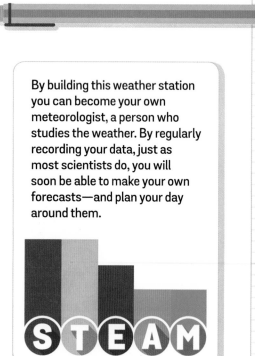

By building this weather station you can become your own meteorologist, a person who studies the weather. By regularly recording your data, just as most scientists do, you will soon be able to make your own forecasts—and plan your day around them.

WEATHER TEMPLATE

Date	10/21
Time	10:20 a.m.
Temperature	60°F/15°C
Barometric pressure	30.31
Humidity	High
Precipitation type and amount	Rain ¼ in. (6 mm)
Wind direction	NW
Wind speed	Low

What You'll Need . . .

- 3 "louvered" cupboard doors about 24 in. (61 cm) high and 12 in. (30 cm) wide
- Plywood scraps for the base, back, and roof (size to suit the louvered doors)
- 4 wooden battens 71 in. (180 cm) long plus a selection of scraps
- Piece of cord about 24 in. (61 cm) long
- Hinges
- White paint
- Thin plastic sheet
- Hammer, handsaw, cordless drill/driver, and scissors

1. Take two of the doors (one for each side of the cabinet) and screw a batten to each of the vertical edges.

2. Link the two sides with a base, back, and roof made from plywood. Make sure there's a generous all-around overhang on the roof, with the highest end of the slope being at the front over the door. Use scraps to strengthen the "legs" as in the picture.

3. The front door of the cabinet is made from the third louvered door and is hinged at the bottom with a piece of cord attached like a castle drawbridge. When horizontal it is used for a surface to work on.

4. Paint the box white. Tack thin plastic sheet over the roof to keep the rain out, and put the instruments inside (apart from the rain gauge and wind vane, which need to be attached on top).

The Instruments

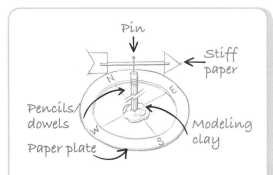

Weather/Windvane

A simple instrument that rotates with the wind and points to the wind direction (North, South, East or West).

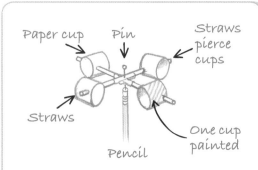

Anemometer

This is a windmill-like instrument that is used to indicate wind speed; the faster it spins the stronger the wind.

Hygrometer

A hygrometer is used for measuring humidity, which is the amount of moisture present in the air. Daily hygrometer observations will enable you to record humidity patterns that will in turn help you to forecast the weather.

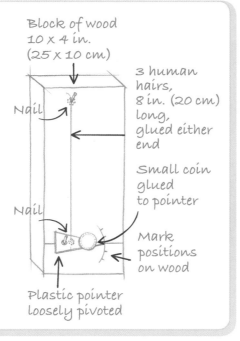

Block of wood
10 x 4 in.
(25 x 10 cm)

3 human hairs,
8 in. (20 cm) long,
glued either end

Small coin glued to pointer

Nail

Nail

Mark positions on wood

Plastic pointer loosely pivoted

Rain Gauge

This is an instrument used for measuring rainfall. The diameter of the vessel or "capture cup" and the scale that shows the depth of the captured water will enable you to measure how much rain has fallen over the last 24-hour period.

Barometer

A barometer is an instrument used to measure atmospheric (air) pressure. High pressure indicates clear weather, and low pressure means clouds and rain. When you see your barometer readings going down as the air pressure falls, it's likely to rain; if they are going up, the sun will probably shine.

12 in. (30 cm) long tube with water sucked up to halfway and sealed off

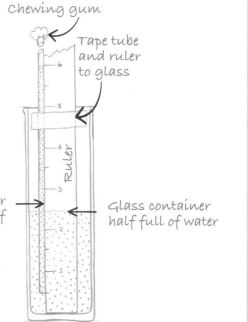

Chewing gum

Tape tube and ruler to glass

Ruler

Glass container half full of water

Eco Go

One of the most important days of my life was when I learned to ride a bicycle.

—Michael Palin, English comedian and traveler (1943–)

Eco Bicycling

Your "eco bike" can have whatever you want, but be sure to fit it with dynamo lights, a solar power pack, and a trailer. An eco bike is a means of transport that doesn't damage the environment. You could let your parents drive you all over the place in their car, but what's the point in wasting precious energy and smogging up the atmosphere when you can turn your wheels into a 21st-century, self-sufficient, energy-efficient, low-carbon, green machine? The humble bicycle has never been so cool!

Why Is an Eco Bike "Low-Carbon?"

Apart from the initial energy costs involved in the production of the bike, and in transporting it from wherever in the world it was made to a shop near you, your bike costs little or nothing to run. You don't need to buy any fuel and cycling doesn't produce polluting fumes. It's an altogether clean, carbon-mean machine.

Will It Cost Lots of Money?

One visit to the local dump and talking with various family friends and neighbors provided us with a couple of bikes for spare parts, two dynamos, a solar power generator, and a whole heap of bits and pieces. There's a lot of interest these days in swapping bikes, bits of bikes, and all things bikey. This means that it needn't cost very much at all, even to get the bike itself in the first place.

How Is It Cool?

As a kid I had an old army bike. My sons were not so lucky (my youngest had to make do with a ladies' folding bike!). Nowadays, though, even cheap bikes are amazing, with front and rear suspension and at least ten gears. Look on the internet, or go down to your local bike shop, and see what eco additions you can stick on. How about a chopper bike with flashing solar lights, or a mountain bike with wind turbines on the handlebars for recharging your phone and media player? Why not customize a pedal go-kart for your younger brother or sister? Just use your imagination to invent stuff for your bike.

Dynamo

Some clever kids use a dynamo to charge a battery, which means you won't be without lights when you are stationary (this is a major drawback of dynamo lights). Look on the internet and see what you can find out about doing that.

1. The simplest option is to fit a "rub-on-wheel" dynamo, as shown in the photograph on the right. So first get hold of one of these, and a pair of bicycle lights (one for the front and one for the back).

2. Study your dynamo, and the style and shape of your bike, and see how best it can be fitted on the front or back wheel without any danger of it getting in the way of the brakes, pedals, and chain.

3. Clamp the dynamo to the frame so that when in the "off" position it's clear of the tire, and when in the "on" position it's pressed hard against the tire.

4. Attach the front and back lights to the bike.

5. With the frame acting as one "wire," link the lights and the dynamo up with the other wire. Now when you turn the dynamo on and ride your bike the lights should work, powered by your legs!

Here you'll use dynamo technology to create sustainable power, only this time, instead of solar or wind, you'll be generating electricity by the power of your own two legs! Include a battery (optional) and you'll get practice with storing the electricity you make so that you can use it later.

It should press against the tire, but only when in the "on" position.

Solar PV Charger

A solar photovoltaic (PV) charger, as shown in the photo below and the diagram on page (123), is inexpensive to buy and will power all your mobile electronics—phone, music player, digital camera, and so on. The charger converts and stores solar energy so that you can plug into it when one of your pieces of equipment needs topping up. When it comes to fitting it, think about how you use your bike and then attach the charger so that it can easily be removed. If you have brackets for it both at the front and back of the bike, you'll be able to move the charger to take advantage of the position of the sun.

To supplement the muscle-powered dynamo (see opposite page), you can set your bike up to also collect energy passively, without requiring work, by adding a small solar panel. More exposure to photovoltaic technology will give you a better understanding of how solar energy can help you out, especially when you're traveling and away from any wall outlets.

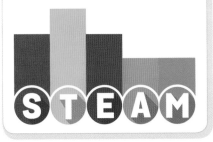

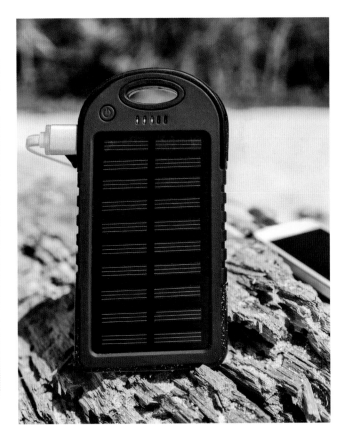

Eco Bike Trailer

What You'll Need . . .

- 9 x 71 in. (180 cm) lengths of ¾ in. (18 mm) diameter bamboo, and/or lightweight metal tubing
- Tools such as tape measure, handsaw, hacksaw, hammer, drill, pliers, and sandpaper
- Mild steel about ⅛ in. (3 mm) thick for the two axle brackets and the universal joint
- Flexible metal cable—the sort that you can get from a chandlers (a shop that sells stuff for boats) with 4 metal cable grips (to grip the return end of cable when forming a loop)
- Box, net, rack, or seat
- 2 bicycle wheels of about the same diameter as the ones on your bike
- 50 bolts, ¼ in. (6 mm) in diameter, 6½ in. (16.5 cm) long, with washers and nuts to fit. These bolts are cut to length as required.

Mother Nature can be high tech, too: bamboo is lightweight, strong, and completely sustainable. To make your trailer really useful, you'll need to do some engineering work to ensure it can comfortably support heavy loads.

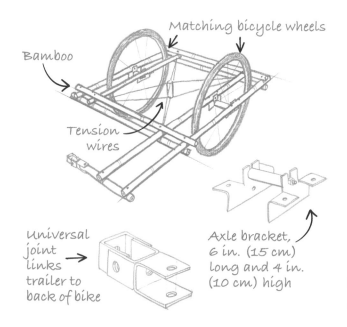

Matching bicycle wheels

Bamboo

Tension wires

Universal joint links trailer to back of bike

Axle bracket, 6 in. (15 cm) long and 4 in. (10 cm) high

1. Have a look at the photograph below and the drawings, and collect together the material you are likely to use. The trailer is made from bamboo, old bike wheels, and some bits and bobs that can be bought or made from scratch.

2. Carefully cut, drill, and bolt together the nine lengths of bamboo that form the basic frame of the trailer. Sizes depend on how big or small you want the trailer to be, so you decide.

3. Make the axle brackets. Cut to size with a hacksaw, bend to shape with a hammer, drill holes as shown opposite, and bolt them to the bamboo frame.

4. Make or buy the universal joint that links the trailer to the bike (opposite). This is made from 3 identical pieces of metal 6 in. (15 cm) long and 2 in. (5 cm) wide, drilled and bent into U–shapes. Attach it to the trailer frame.

5. Fix metal cables across the diagonals of the frame using the cable grips at the ends and bolts through the frame.

6. Attach a box, net, rack, or seat to the trailer, depending on what you are going to carry.

7. Fit the wheels, attach the universal joint to your bike's rear wheel spindle, and you're ready for an adventure.

Testing out the design in the school car parking lot.

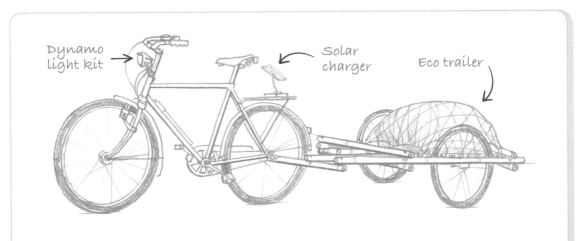

Dynamo light kit

Solar charger

Eco trailer

This bamboo trailer was designed by bike trailer company Carry Freedom and made by students.

Fix a Puncture

When I was a kid cycling to school with my friends, the country roads were so bad that we often got flat tires. We were so well equipped and practiced, though, that we flipped the bike over, repaired it and in ten minutes had it back on the road.

Punctures are usually caused by nails, pins and thorns, and the repair is just a rubber patch stuck over the hole. You can make an inner tube last for many years, and that is the great thing about a bike generally—it's so easy and cheap to repair.

You don't need to be strong, or have extra-big hands, massive thumbs or a huge brain—a simple puncture repair is one of those things that most kids can do. Don't try to do it too quickly until you understand the technique and how to use the rubber solution (the glue that sticks the patch on). If you rush, you'll risk nicking the inner tube with the tire lever (another puncture to mend!) or wasting a patch if you don't get the preparation right.

Knowing your way around a bicycle tire repair kit will give you ease of mind when you travel by bicycle, and after using it once or twice you will know the functions of the parts of the modern tire.

Although this puncture-repair kit is a bit old-fashioned, it gives you a good idea of what you'll need to fix your own bike (see page 126).

Think of
bicycles as
rideable art that can
just about save the world.

—Grant Petersen, American bicycle designer and author (1954–)

What You'll Need . . .

- Puncture–repair kit
- 2–3 tire levers
- Spanner to fit the wheel bolt
- Small amount of water
- Bicycle pump

1. Turn the bike upside down and use the spanner to remove the wheel or if space allows work with the wheel in place.

2. Slip the flat end of the tire lever between the rim and the tire and pull down until you can hook the end of the lever on a spoke. Repeat this with the other levers until one side of the tire is free from the rim.

3. Pull out the inner tube, and remove whatever has caused the puncture.

4. Pump the tube up slightly, and listen, look and feel for escaping air. You might need to wet the tube, in which case you should look for bubbles rather than listen for air.

5. Once you have found and marked the hole, dry the tube, rub the area around the hole with sandpaper, and smear a large coin–sized blob of glue over and around the hole.

6. Wait until the glue has gone dull in appearance, then press the patch in place and leave it for about ten minutes.

7. Finally, push the inner tube back into the tire, ease the tire back onto the rim, refit the wheel, and pump up the tire.

6

Take Eco Action:
Bike While Away from Home

Get on Your Bike ... or Just Rent One

It's not always easy to take a bike with you when you go on vacation or visit friends or family, but the good news is that most cities and big towns have created systems where you can rent a bike for the day. In one small town, there's a man who recycles old cycles. The idea is that a visitor buys one of his bikes at a giveaway price, uses it for a week or so, simply leaves it at the side of the road, and then gives the guy a ring to tell him where it is so that he can go and collect it and recycle it again.

Rental bikes on Times Square, New York.

Which Is Best in the City—Bike, Car, or Subway?

In most cities, it's much easier and quicker to cycle short distances than to spend ages stuck in a car in a traffic jam, or to buy a ticket, stand on a station platform, line up for a place in a hot, sweaty subway train, and then have to stand up for the whole journey if no seats are available.

Take Eco Action:
Drive Cleaner Cars, Drive Less

Can We Ever Do without Cars?

There's really no good reason why we can't figure out how to live without cars, or better still, invent a car that doesn't puff out huge amounts of poisonous emissions. This is what many people are trying to do (see the ideas described on the opposite page), but at the moment a "green" car seems a long way off for many of us. Why not try thinking about how you would go about making the world a car-free place?

Pollution from Cars

- Cars produce toxic waste that damages our health.

- Road transport produces hydrocarbons, nitrogen dioxide, carbon monoxide, metals, and a variety of organic compounds— all dangerous.

- Air pollution from transport produces acid rain, which damages crops, trees, our lungs, and almost everything else.

Vegetable Oil, Hydrogen, or Poo—Which Does Your Car Use?

Probably none of the above! No doubt your car, like most of them, runs on diesel or gasoline (see opposite page for the facts about how much damage these cause). Yet, with any luck, we are just a step away from greener cars that will run on "clean" forms of fuel such as vegetable oil or hydrogen. Many years ago, a chicken farmer called Harold Bate invented a car that would run on chicken manure, so anything's possible!

Strange but True—Cars That Produce Nothing but Water

Water is made up of two parts hydrogen and one part oxygen (that's what "H_2O" means), and we can use electricity to separate the hydrogen from the oxygen. If we reverse the procedure, we can get the electricity back—a bit like what happens on a space shuttle. So, if we were to use fuel cells that use hydrogen and oxygen to create electricity to run the engine, we could have electric cars that give off nothing more toxic than pure water as an emission!

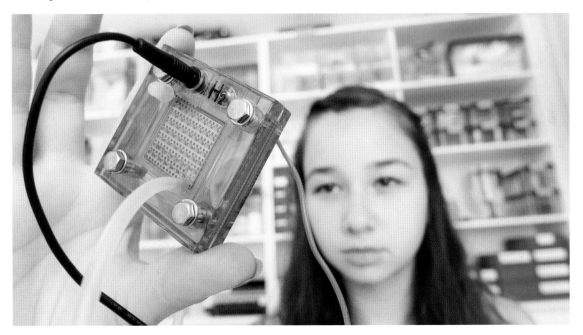

Bike Adventure

One summer, when I was about 11 years old, my grandpa and I decided to cycle about 25 miles to the nearest seaside. It was great. We told gran where we were going, strapped a tent and our sleeping bags onto our bikes, and we were off. Of course, it was hard work—I was small and my grandpa was old—and we were both completely exhausted at the end of the journey, but it was a huge adventure!

How Far in a Day?

If you're eager and fit, you could walk about 10–12 miles (16–19 km) in a day, but give you a bike and, allowing for regular stops for food, rest, and toilet breaks, you could easily cycle about 30–60 miles (50–100 km). Of course, these figures are only rough estimates, and a lot would depend on your bike, your age, and your fitness, but the amazing thing is that a bike allows you to do all this distance with little or no extra effort. I think that cycling is much easier than walking—what do you think?

Planning a bike adventure is a creative process that involves strategic thinking. Study maps, calculate distances, and decide where you'd like to take breaks along the way. Then, while you're on your adventure, don't forget to commemorate the occasion by taking pictures and/or journaling about the new sights you're seeing.

What You'll Need . . .

- You must go with a loving and caring adult.
- Leave a detailed note describing your route and stop-off points.
- Take your phone with you.
- It's more fun if you go in a group with brothers, sisters, and/or friends.
- Make sure your bike is in good, safe condition—it should be well oiled, with good lights and brakes.
- Pack a puncture-repair outfit: puncture kit, tire levers, spanner, and pump (see pages 124–126).
- Take plenty of drinking water.
- Plan a route that uses small country roads and cycle routes, and avoid busy roads (you're not allowed on some big roads).
- Don't cycle after dark.
- Plan well ahead so that you have a good idea of how long it will take you to get to where you are going.
- Make sure you have adequate clothes for the likely weather.
- Make sure you have good maps.
- Cycle in single file and never leave any members of your group behind either when you move off after a stop or during the ride.

The clearest way into the universe is through a forest wilderness.

— John Muir, Scottish–American naturalist and author (1838–1914)

Cycling to School

It's official—cycling is good for your brain! It will also improve your fitness. Sometimes, though, it is just too far to cycle to school, or too dangerous (maybe because of the high number of parents driving their kids to school)—but what is too far or too dangerous? Anything over 8 km (5 miles) is probably too far, and the danger aspect is something you need to discuss with mom or dad.

Fun

Cycling is healthy, good for the environment, and low in cost, but above all it is just good fun. If you asked all your friends, family and neighbors what, when they were kids, was the one thing that really made a difference to their lives, most people would say that it was getting their first bike. Think about it—one moment you're limited to walking, going on a bus, or being driven around in the family car, and the next you're whizzing off all over the place on your trusty bike.

Asthma

If you're an asthma sufferer, you may wonder if cycling is a good idea, with all those hills and car fumes. Sadly, car fumes are bad for everyone's health, especially asthma sufferers, but you could use an anti-pollution mask while you're cycling. On the plus side, though, more bikes equal fewer harmful emissions, and doctors recommend moderate exercise for asthma sufferers as a way of building strength and fitness and helping their lungs.

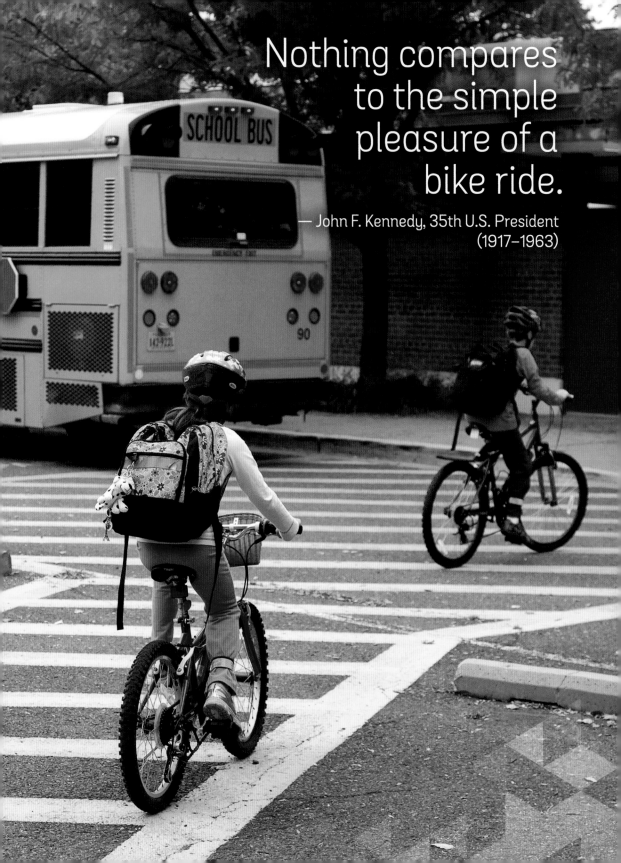

Nothing compares to the simple pleasure of a bike ride.

— John F. Kennedy, 35th U.S. President (1917–1963)

Eco Go-Kart

A go-kart or "soapbox cart" is, in its simplest form, a cart made from four wheels, a plank and a box or seat. If you think an eco go-kart (without an engine) is a bit boring, then think again. Building the kart is fun, and racing it downhill is even more exciting.

When you get confident, maybe you could take part in an official race and even get a trophy! Then, if you want to try something a bit more advanced, you can have a go at racing a wind-powered "land yacht" or "kite buggy."

In the old days, people made and repaired just about everything—long before terms like "eco" and "recycling" were in common usage. With go-karts, the eco challenge is seeing if you can make one totally from recycled materials. If you succeed, it will give you so much more pleasure and enjoyment than if you just went out and bought one. Also, if it breaks down, you will know exactly how to repair it, since you were the one who made it in the first place!

On the surface this project couldn't be simpler: it has four wheels and rolls downhill or when pushed. But because of all the different looks that can be achieved it will allow you to really get creative. Since you'll want your cart to roll as fast as possible, you'll want to limit friction, a major focus of mechanical engineering and Newtonian physics.

Designing Your Kart

Your kart can be as big or small, as basic or fancy, as your materials and skills allow—and that's where the fun begins. If you search "soapbox carts," you'll see that there are some miraculous designs out there. One person has made a cart entirely from old washing machines. If you're really interested, you could see if you could get your craft, design, and technology department at school involved, and set up a race.

How Much Will It Cost?

Apart from the price of a few nuts and bolts, and the fuel costs involved in driving to collect bits and pieces from friends, family and the local dump, our kart (see page 136) cost almost nothing. The best thing to do is find the wheels first—after that you're cruising.

There is no such thing as "away." When we throw anything away, it must go somewhere.

— Annie Leonard, American sustainability proponent and filmmaker (1964–)

What You'll Need...

- The whole point of this project is to use salvaged wood but here are some dimensions to use as a guide: one plank of wood or piece of plywood 36 in. (92 cm) long, 18 in. (46 cm) wide, and 1 in. (2.5 cm) thick plus 4 planks of wood 36 in. (92 cm) long, 6 in. (15 cm) wide and ¾ in. (18 mm) thick
- 2 metal ½ in. (12 mm) threaded rods, 40 in. (100 cm) long with 8 washers and 4 nuts to fit

- Large 5 in. (13 cm) bolt, with a nut and 3 washers
- Child's car seat
- 2 small bike wheels
- 2 trolley wheels
- Rope, 79 in. (200 cm) long
- Tools and materials such as cordless drill/driver and bits, handsaw, hammer, tape measure, nails, screws, bolts, washers, and nuts

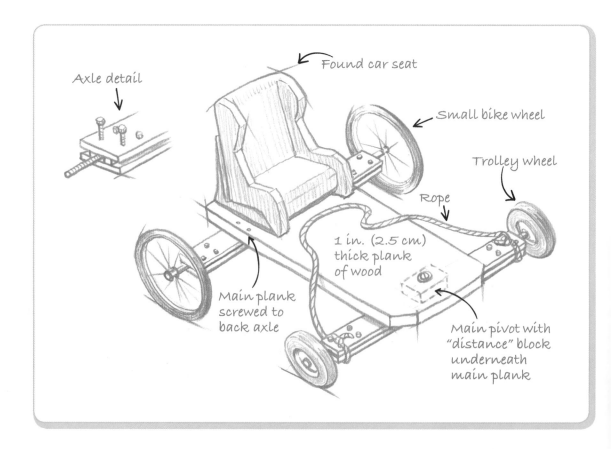

Axle detail

Found car seat

Small bike wheel

Trolley wheel

Rope

1 in. (2.5 cm) thick plank of wood

Main plank screwed to back axle

Main pivot with "distance" block underneath main plank

1. Sit down on the ground with your legs bent and braced—just as if you were sitting on a kart—and get a friend to measure the distance from the back of your seat to your feet. Allowing for a little extra at front and back, use a handsaw to cut the main plank to length.

2. Make the back axle by sandwiching one of the metal rods between two narrow planks. Then screw the whole thing to the main plank so that you finish up with a large T shape.

3. Make the front axle as you did the back one. Position it so that it crosses beneath the front end of the main plank. Use a block of waste wood as a distance piece sandwiched between the plank and the front axle (see diagram opposite). Then drill a large pivot hole through the center of the plank, the block, and the front axle.

4. With the main plank resting on the block and axle, pass the large bolt through the pivot hole, making sure you have one or more washers between the layers of wood. Then use two or more nuts to fix the bolt so that it's secure but still allows the front axle to be turned.

5. Screw the seat firmly to the back end of the main plank.

6. Fit the four wheels onto the ends of the axles. Put washers each side of the wheels, fit the nuts, and hammer over the ends of the axle rods (to stop the nuts from coming off).

7. Drill two holes—one at each end of the front-axle planks—and use them to tie the steering rope firmly in place. Now all you need is someone to push you along!

Karting Rules

Keep off public roads is the main rule. The best place to use your kart is in your own yard or nearest park. For more variety, try private land with the owners' permission (they will tell you if it's safe) or on a beach. Also, think what may happen if the kart runs out of your control. Don't use it near pedestrians, obstacles, or areas that may be dangerous. Also, never use the kart for stunts.

Take Eco Action:
Fly Less

Why is it that most of the people who tell us that air travel is much cleaner than road transportation—so clean that really it doesn't matter—are involved in some way with aircraft companies and travel organizations? Air travel is making our dirty air even dirtier. So it's a good idea to think about how we can still have great vacations without the need to fly.

Are Vacations Near Home Any Good?

Just imagine swimming and snorkeling in the sea, pottering among rock pools, lying flat down in a field and looking up at the night sky, sleeping in a tent with a friend, picnicking, biking—vacations at home are only as good or as bad as you make them. OK, maybe you live in a city and you're short on cash, but what's to stop you and a group of friends from outfitting yourselves with tents and backpacks and going on a walking and camping trip in the nearest bit of beautiful countryside? Talk to your friends, parents, and teachers—they'll have plenty of ideas to inspire you. Do remember though, that if you go on a trip, you must go with a loving and caring adult.

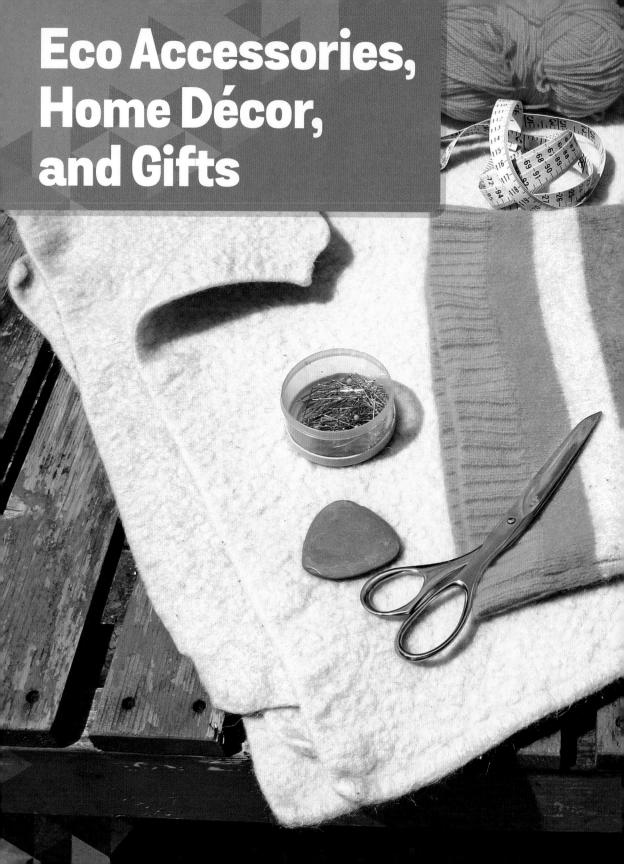

Eco Accessories, Home Décor, and Gifts

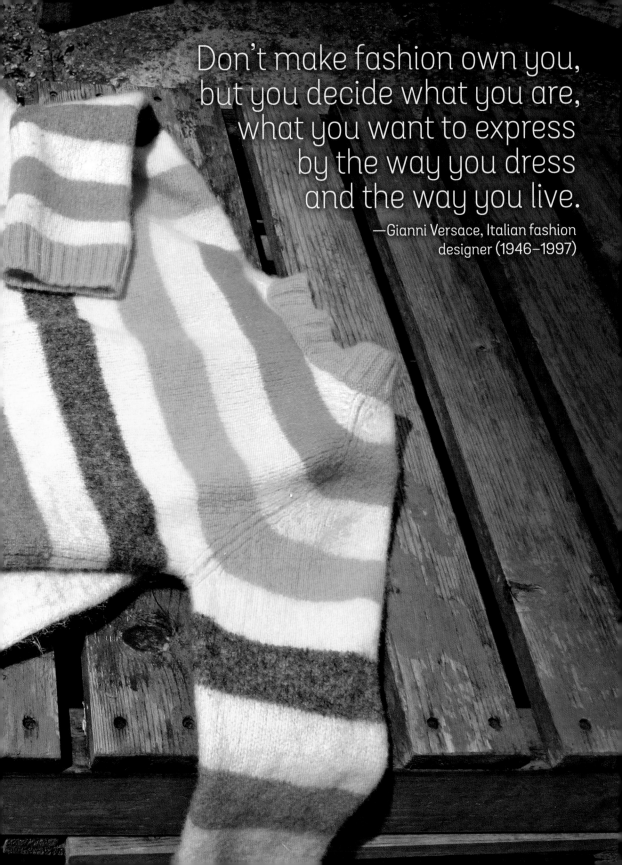

Don't make fashion own you,
but you decide what you are,
what you want to express
by the way you dress
and the way you live.

—Gianni Versace, Italian fashion
designer (1946–1997)

Eco Bangles

Why trash the environment even more by wasting money on a useless gift? Eco bangles are the same type of jewelry that used to be called "bling," but made cheaply from recycled waste materials—things that might otherwise be thrown away. And because you're custom-building the jewelry, you can tailor it to suit someone's style.

You can make eco bangles from just about any stuff that comes your way—old coins, bits of broken watches and clocks, bottle caps, electronic components, cogs from old engines, cleaned-up spark plugs, bits from an old socket spanner set . . . anything you like the look of and is OK for you to use. Always check with an adult first in case something is too valuable, sharp, pointed, or toxic to be suitable. Never use anything that could cause an injury.

I chose to make this example of an eco bracelet (at right) from a collection of key rings, marine chain shackles and swivels, metal washers, and coins with holes in the center, for six good reasons. I like the feel of high-quality metal components (the sort of thing you would see in a chandlers and/or in engineers' workshops), I have always collected such items, I like the weight, they won't rust or tarnish, they can be put together in various ways, and they can be swiftly taken apart and reused when I want to go on to other things.

Because its outcome depends only on what materials are available to you and how you use them, this project is purely creative. Enjoy the process of making jewelry that is meaningful to you and cost-free to the environment.

Eco bangles can be as big, bold, and cool as you want to make them.

REMEMBER:
Always check with an adult first in case something is too valuable, sharp, pointed, or toxic to be suitable. Never use anything that could cause an injury!

Native American Button Bracelet

Long ago, when Europeans first settled in America, their everyday items were of great interest to the Native American peoples, because they were so different to their own handcrafted items. American native and cowboy costumes of the late 19th century often included highly decorative bracelets, bangles, and necklaces made from these everyday items, such as coins, mirrors, glass beads, copper wire, buttons, and brightly colored fabrics.

When my great grandmother died, my grandmother inherited her button box, and then when she died my mum inherited her buttons. Buttons are great examples of good eco recycling, in that they are used and reused over many generations. Old buttons are also part of our historical heritage—I have some brass buttons that my grandfather wore on his uniform when he was a fireman in London during the wartime "Blitz" in the early 1940s, and a button that my great grandfather carved from a piece of whalebone.

You will have success with this project if you balance the materials you have against some research into Native American art history, to create an eye-catching arrangement. Plus, working out patterns of colors and/or shapes flexes the mathematical part of your brain.

Choosing buttons and working out their pattern will give you a fun chance to express your creativity. You'll learn a bit about Native American culture, too, by researching their jewelry and traditions.

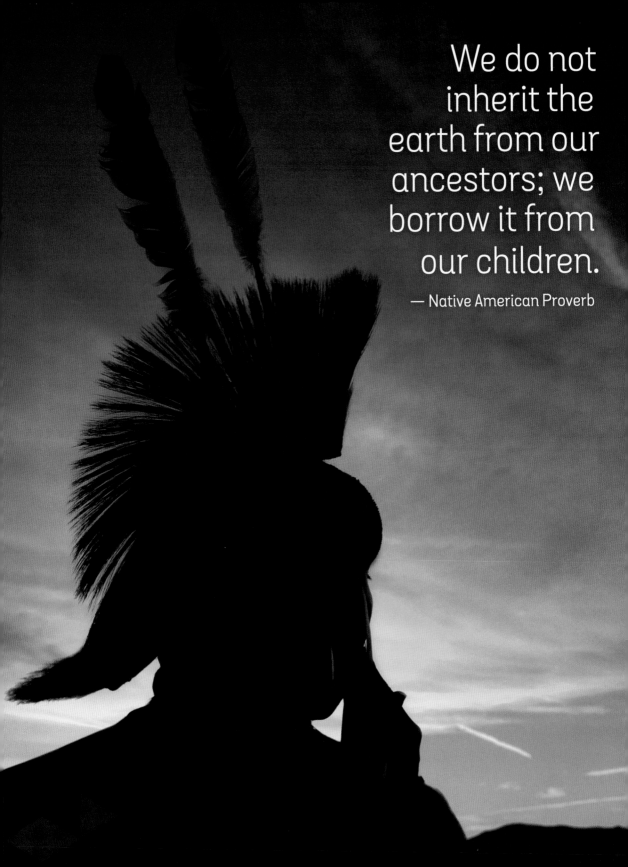

We do not inherit the earth from our ancestors; we borrow it from our children.

— Native American Proverb

What You'll Need ...

- Two large needles
- Strong thread
- Buttons

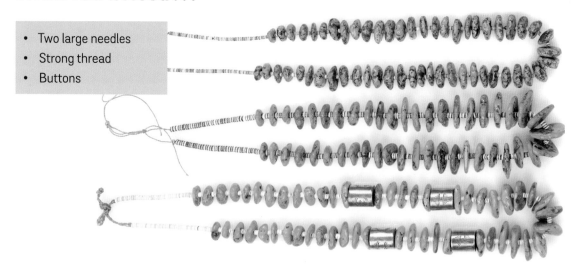

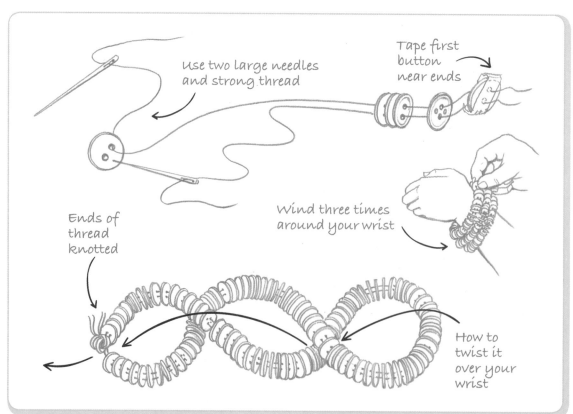

Use two large needles and strong thread

Tape first button near ends

Wind three times around your wrist

Ends of thread knotted

How to twist it over your wrist

Where Can You Get Buttons and Ideas?

Start by asking all your relations and friends, and then look around garage sales, church sales, and flea markets. Don't forget that some buttons are valuable. For example, one of the pearl-like buttons we used in our bracelet is in fact a real pearl from a hatpin, the sort of thing ladies wore every day a few generations ago.

A quick look on the internet at pictures of Native American costumes will show you that buttons were used in much the same way as beads. They were threaded onto cords and/or bone pins and rods to make both curved and straight jewelry—things like bangles, headdress bands, and belts. Start by sorting your buttons into similar types—same color, same shape, same material—and then simply experiment by putting them on two strands of strong thread or elastic until you're happy with the result.

Felt Shoulder Bag

Felt is a type of cloth that is made by mashing and squeezing bits of wooly fleece until it matts together. The wool could come from a sheep, a goat, a llama, or even a yak. Almost all other fabrics are woven or knitted, but if you could travel back in time 6,000 years to Turkey you would find that felt was all they used. Nomadic Mongolians nowadays use felt for clothes, shoes, hats, and yurts (their houses). The green material on billiard tables is made from felt. Cowboy hats were also made out of felt.

Felt is very eco-friendly. It more or less lasts forever, it's made from natural materials, and it has unique insulating qualities. You can make it from old woolen blankets, sweaters, and scarves—perhaps even that horrible sweater your aunt knitted for you (you know you can't throw it away, but maybe it could shrink in the wash and then get recycled . . .).

From the materials to the patterns to the decorations, this shoulder bag gives you plenty of chances to make design choices that express how you feel. You will also gain a basic knowledge of threading materials together to make something really attractive and handy at the same time.

What You'll Need . . .

- A single-bed-sized 100% wool blanket (we got ours from a charity shop) and a brightly colored, knitted 100% wool sweater for pockets or decoration
- Thin or tracing paper

- Brightly colored woolen yarn to complement the colors of the sweater and/or blanket
- Household items such as scissors, tape measure, buttons, chalk, hole punch, pins, needles, sewing cotton and large darning needle

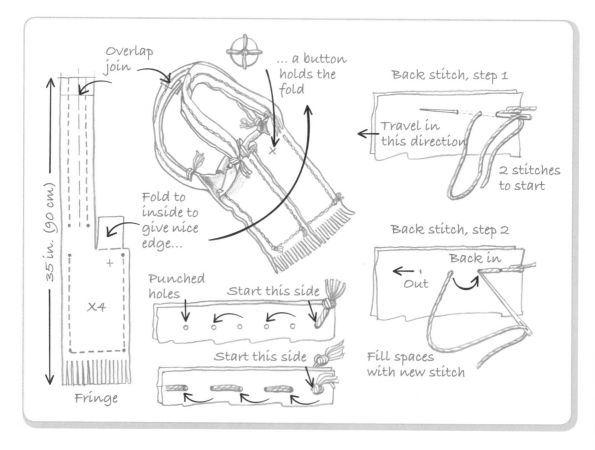

1. Put your old 100% wool item in the washing machine, add powder or liquid, and wash on the hottest setting. It will shrink to about half to one-third of its original size. A blanket will make a big bag and a sweater a small one.

2. Choose a scale (size) that allows you to get four identical pieces from your fabric using the pattern above. Transfer the pattern to thin paper, trim it to shape, pin it onto the shrunken fabric and cut it out. Repeat until you have four identical shapes.

3. "Tack" these identical shapes together (using big temporary stitches) and use colored chalk to mark in the position of the final stitch holes, about 1 in. (2.5 cm) apart. Use a hole punch to make holes for these stitches.

4. Double up the woolen yarn twice so that it is four strands thick, and sew the felt cutouts together with large, in-and-out stitches. Work right around in one direction, and when you get to the starting point change direction—so that you fill in the blanks on the return run. Or use back stitch as shown.

5. Finally, remove the tacking stitches, add pockets and decoration. Fold the edge flaps as shown in the diagram and photo and hold them in place with a button.

Inspired by Native American Warrior Wear

If you were to put your favorite super-smooth 100% wool sweater in the washing machine and run a high-temperature program by mistake, the item would shrink to about half the size, the texture would be thick and lumpy, the colors would run and blur, it would be super-strong—and you would be very upset!

The good news is that you can use this "felting" effect to create a really cool bag. We got the idea for this design from a Native American bag—the sort that a warrior wore on his back. If that's too macho, and you'd prefer it to be more pink and sparkly or catwalk chic, then just get your pens out and design your own eco bag. If bags aren't your thing, I am sure someone you know needs a bag-for-life for their weekly shopping—imagine how impressed they will be! Before you start, though, make sure that the woollen items you intend to use are not precious to someone.

Patchwork Rag Bag

Most of us have seen old patchwork quilts and cushions made out of hundreds of little hexagonal scraps of fabric. These scraps were all sewn together with incredibly small hand stitches, and the results are quite amazing. Patchwork using rags, however, is quite different. The patchwork is made from torn strips of fabric, with the torn edges fully on view, and the whole thing is put together on a sewing machine, which saves a lot of time.

We own a piece of patchwork, made over 100 years ago by an ancestor of ours, that uses all sorts of bits from worn-out clothes. Finding a new life for old clothes is even better than putting them in the recycle bin.

Mastering a sewing machine will take your knowledge of useful household tools further; the look and feel of the bag itself is something that you decide based on where you source your materials. You'll get to know textiles as an artistic medium.

What You'll Need . . .

- A selection of fabrics
- Backing fabric that is twice the size of the bag that you want to make
- 2 lengths of strong braid or belt material for the handle straps
- Sewing machine
- Household items such as scissors, tape measure, chalk, pins, needles and sewing cotton

1. Tear your chosen fabric into about 34 strips, each about 35 in. (90 cm) long and 2 in. (5 cm) wide. Don't worry about the frayed edges, or if the strips vary in width along their length.

2. Set the sewing machine to zigzag, and stitch the strips onto a piece of backing fabric that is about 20 in. (50 cm) wide and 35 in. (90 cm) long—this will make a bag 20 in. (50 cm) wide and 16–18 in. (40–45 cm) deep. Here the strips are running down the length of the fabric, but there's no reason why you can't go for another direction or have overlapping strips.

3. Fold the ends of the backing fabric over so that the ends of the torn strips are covered up, and fix the folded flaps in place with zigzag stitches.

4. Fold the whole thing in half so that you have the bag shape, and set the shape by running a line of zigzag stitches about 1 in. (2.5 cm) in from the edges of the sides.

5. Take two lengths of strap for the handles, pin them in place at either side edge of the bag, and fix them in place with a rectangular shape of zigzag stitches. Use cotton of a contrasting color for a bold effect.

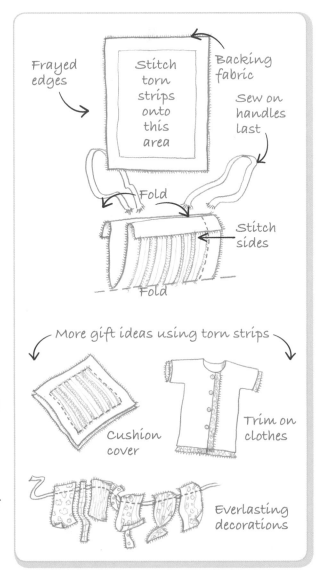

Frayed edges

Stitch torn strips onto this area

Backing fabric

Sew on handles last

Fold

Stitch sides

Fold

More gift ideas using torn strips

Cushion cover

Trim on clothes

Everlasting decorations

Take Eco Action:
Waste Less

What Happens to All the Waste?

In the developed world, we each throw out our own bodyweight in trash every 6–7 weeks. We do recycle things like glass and metal, but for the most part we either bury or burn our rubbish. The buried stuff oozes out poisons for several lifetimes afterwards, while the burnt stuff fills the air we breathe with huge amounts of toxic fumes.

Should We Buy Less?

One look around yard or garage sale shows that the world is sinking in a sea of rubbish—plastic toys, cell phones, old clothes, and so on. The more we have, the more we want, and we always want the latest model, discarding the previous one even if it's not broken. So the answer is yes!

Postage–Stamp Bowl

"Philately decoupage" is the fancy name for this technique, but it only means decorating things with postage stamps! "Philately" is the study and collection of postage stamps, and "decoupage" is the craft of decorating objects with paper cutouts.

Decoupage has always been eco-friendly, simply because the craft uses saved paper (in this case postage stamps) to create decorative items. If you don't think that postage stamps are very exciting, there's no reason why you can't use pictures printed out from your computer, bubble–gum wrappers, fruit wrappers or labels from your favorite food instead—in fact, you can use anything as long as it's made of printed paper. Remember that some postage stamps are worth huge amounts of money, so it would be better not to use those for this project!

It's all art here. The decisions you make about (a) what blank canvas, or backing object, to use, (b) what reusable decoupage medium, or material, you layer on the substrate, and (c) how you arrange your stamps—by color, by shape, or by something else—will show you the steps necessary to complete a mixed-media art project.

What You'll Need . . .

- Plastic or wooden bowl
- Sandpaper
- Stamps
- Water in a spray container
- PVA glue
- 1–4 cm (½–1½ in.) paintbrush
- Water-based high-shine varnish

1. Take a found plastic or wooden bowl and use a piece of sandpaper to rub it down to a slightly matt (roughened) finish.

2. Spray your postage stamps with water to make them thoroughly damp.

3. Give the whole bowl, inside and out, a coat of PVA glue—the sort of glue that you use to stick wood, paper and fabric.

4. Take your dampened stamps and use the PVA glue to stick them one at a time to the bowl. Make sure that the stamps are pressed firmly down, with no raised corners or air bubbles.

5. Continue until every part of the bowl has been covered.

6. Finally, when the whole thing is completely dry, give it several coats of high-shine varnish and the task is finished.

What Can You Cover With Decoupage?

You can decorate just about anything that has a firm and permanent surface. Small items, such as a box, bowl, dish, book or picture, are a good starting point, and for a more ambitious project try a chair, side table or mirror. Decoupage screens are also good.

Knitted Bedspread

The greatest thing about our lovely knitted patchwork bedspread is that it's totally eco-friendly. It's completely handmade (no carbon-producing machines or motors are needed), it uses loads of recycled wool, and, best of all, once finished it will keep you really warm as well as looking pretty. It's fun to make and to use!

Is Knitting Easy?

Basic hand knitting is very easy. All you need is the wool or yarn, a pair of knitting needles and a few basic tips, and you'll be well away. The best way of learning is to have one-on-one lessons—someone in your family will most likely be a first-class knitter. Here are some interesting facts and figures to think about:

- Knitting was once a macho activity—the sort of thing that soldiers and sailors did between battles.

- Knitting helps the brain work—it's good for math and for hand-eye coordination.

- There are over 24 million keen knitters in the USA alone—so how many do you think there might be in the whole world?

The link between knitting and math is now firmly established, as experts acknowledge that what knitters do is think in high-level mathematical terms without even knowing it! Indeed, the hands-on, relaxing nature of knitting makes it an appealing tool in STEAM education.

A ball of yarn is the potential to make a dream that you have come true.

— Melanie Falick, American textile artist, writer, and editor

What You'll Need . . .

- Leftover wool
- Pair of US 6 (4 mm) knitting needles
- Tape measure

- Scissors
- Large darning needle
- Thread

HOW TO KNIT

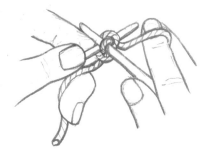

Casting On. Make a loop on the left hand needle and knot loosely to secure. This is the first stitch. Pull through a stitch on the left needle and slip the new loop/stitch onto the left needle.

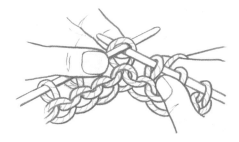

The Knit Stitch 1. Insert the point of the right needle into the stitch on the left needle.

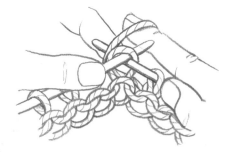

The Knit Stitch 2. With your index finger, wind the yarn under and over the point of the right needle.

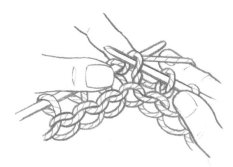

The Knit Stitch 3. Using the right needle, pull the new stitch through the old stitch to form a loop, and slide the old stitch off the left needle onto the right needle.

Practicing the knit stitch.

TIP:
Ask a good knitter to help!

1. Search for leftover wool—try charity shops, friends and family. It's best if the wool is all the same weight and thickness.

2. Find someone who knows how to knit, and ask them to show you a few basic stitches, as well as how to start or "cast on," and how to finish off.

3. Once you can manage a stitch, practice over and over again until you know what you are doing.

4. When you and your mates have knitted a big stack of rectangles—we used 104 rectangles each measuring 10 x 7 in. (25 x 18 cm) (60 stiches, 48 rows)—then you can start sewing them together using a simple back stitch (see page 150) into strips.

5. Finally, once you have sewn 13 rectangles end-to-end to make eight strips, and the eight strips side-to-side to make the blanket, ask an adult to sew a hem all around the blanket to give it strength.

A team effort!

Take Eco Action:
Make and Follow a Plan

Why not discuss your ideas to help the environment with your family and friends? This page lists some things you can take action on immediately, and gives some suggestions for organizations you may like to check out. Imagine what you would like to do in the future to help the environment. Think about the impact your life is going to have on the world around you, and you might improve things.

✔	ACTION	SEE PAGE...
	Use only energy-saving lightbulbs, and turn off lights when not needed	
	Whenever it's safe and practical, use your bike or public transportation to get around	118
	Use the car much less	128
	Avoid packaged food	57
	Don't eat battery chicken or other factory-farmed meat	71
	Don't nag your parents about getting new clothes	155
	Wear warmer clothes in winter to save on heating, and turn down the heat	
	Turn off all standby equipment at night	

Eco Organizations

You may like to have a look at what projects these nonprofit eco organzations have going on. Remember, you MUST ask your parents' advice and permission before joining any organization or signing up for their newsletters, because only your parents will know if it's appropriate for you.

350.org	350.org
Clean Water Action	www.cleanwateraction.org
Greenpeace	www.greenpeace.org
National Wildlife Federation	www.nwf.org
The Nature Conservancy	www.nature.org
Ocean Conservancy	oceanconservancy.org
Rainforest Action Network	www.ran.org
Rainforest Alliance	www.rainforest-alliance.org
Sierra Club	www.sierraclub.org
World Wildlife Fund	www.worldwildlife.org

Furoshiki Wrap

In Japan, a "furoshiki" is a piece of pretty cloth used to carry just about anything. Items that can be carried this way include books, bottles, fruit, documents, clothes, groceries, and gifts. The size, shape, and design of the cloth, and the way the furoshiki is wrapped and knotted, are all very important.

So, for example, a large furoshiki wrap that is used for carrying heavy groceries might be made of stout cotton and knotted so that there are two carrying handles, whereas a fragile present might simply be wrapped in a delicately printed silk. The wonderful thing about a gift that is wrapped in a furoshiki is that the wrapping is considered to be just as important as the gift, and it is reusable.

The quality, texture, and knotting techniques of the furoshiki are first admired, the gift is then unwrapped, and finally the furoshiki cloth is carefully folded and either reused for another gift or employed as a scarf, tablecloth, or whatever might be appropriate.

Following precise folding patterns trains the mathematical part of your brain, while choosing the right color, size, and strength of wrap material for the right gift builds your appreciation for material aesthetics, or making something that is satisfying to the senses of sight and feel.

Meaning

Furoshiki comes from two words—"furo", meaning bath, and "shiki", meaning spread. The complete word was first used in Japan during a time called the "Edo period" when people going to public baths wrapped up their clothes in a special cloth.

How to Use Furoshiki Wrap

Next time you're buying a present for your grandmother, you could get her a box of chocolates and a silk headscarf, and carefully wrap the chocolate box up in the headscarf. Or, if you study the diagrams on the next few pages, you'll see that there are furoshiki wrapping solutions for just about everything, whatever its shape or size.

Furoshiki Examples

SQUARE PRESENT

Step 1

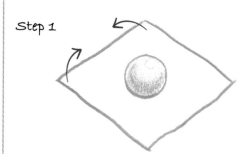

Step 2

Tie
opposite
corners

Step 3

Repeat
with
remaining
corners

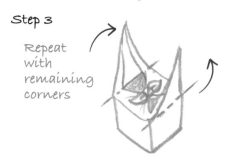

ROUND PRESENT

Step 1

Step 2

Tie
corners
together
to form
loops

Step 3

Pass one
loop through
the other to
make a
carry handle

Step 4

THE KNOT

Pass
corners
around each
other then
back through,
and pull
tight

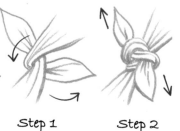

Step 1   Step 2

LONG PRESENT

Step 1

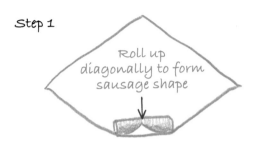

Roll up diagonally to form sausage shape

Step 2

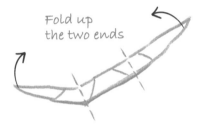

Fold up the two ends

Step 3

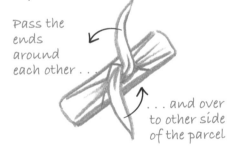

Pass the ends around each other . . .

. . . and over to other side of the parcel

Step 4

Turn it over and tie the ends

TWO BOOKS

Step 1

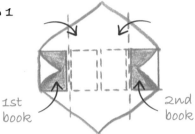

1st book

2nd book

Step 2

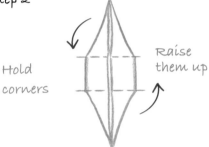

Hold corners

Raise them up

Step 3

Twist the ends around . . .

. . . and turn parcel over

Step 4

Twist and tie to form handles

Books hang downward

Index